T0381869

WILLIAM BOLTS

WILLIAM BOLTS

A DUTCH ADVENTURER
UNDER JOHN COMPANY

BY

N. L. HALLWARD, M.A.

CAMBRIDGE
AT THE UNIVERSITY PRESS
1920

PREFACE

THIS narrative of the life of William Bolts has been written in order to place at the disposal of the historical student a considerable amount of valuable material which has been hitherto not available, or not easily accessible, regarding the relations of the East India Company and its servants with the Country Powers, with the natives of India in general, and with rival European traders during the closing years of the eighteenth century. The publication of the work has been held up for many years—first by the difficulties which at one time hampered research in India, next by the reluctance of publishers to risk the issue of a book which might fail to interest the general public, and lastly by the war. At the same time it is hoped that some parts of the story may be not without interest for the general reader, owing to the light which they throw on the causes of the Patna Massacre and on the extraordinary unpopularity of the Nabobs, or returned Anglo-Indians, which is so widely reflected in early, and even in mid, Victorian literature. The root cause of the trouble was the indefensible system under which the Company paid its servants mere pittances and allowed them to recoup themselves by private trade. As Macaulay insisted, Clive was clearly right in his contention that it was absurd to give men power and require them to live in penury.

It is probable that a search among the archives of Vienna and of Paris would yield further information about the later years of William Bolts's career, of which very little is known from 1784 until his death in 1808.

I am indebted to Mr Wilton J. Bolst for a pedigree of the Bolst or Bolts family from the later years of the eighteenth century to the present day, and for a copy of the death certificate of Mrs Ann Bolts, widow of William Bolts. I have also to thank the Right Rev. Monsignor A. Doubleday, late Rector of St John's Seminary, Wonersh, and the members of his staff, the Rev. J. Costa de Beauregard, of Ore Place, Hastings, and the Rev. C. H. Collins, of the Seminaire des Carmes, Paris, for their kind assistance in elucidating the meaning of a rather obscure French phrase.

N, L. H.

October 1920

CONTENTS

BOOK I

BOOK II

PRESIDENTS AND GOVERNORS
OF FORT WILLIAM, 1758-1772

COL. CLIVE. 1758 (June)

HOLWELL. 1760 (January)

VANSITTART. 1760 (July)

SPENCER. 1764 (December)

LORD CLIVE. 1765 (May)

VERELST. 1767 (January)

CARTIER. 1769 (December)

HASTINGS, GOVERNOR-GENERAL. 1772 (April)

BOOK I

CHAPTER I

APPOINTMENT AND EARLY CAREER IN BENGAL

AMONG the most remarkable civilian adventurers of the eighteenth century in the territories of the East India Company was William Bolts, who by private trade accumulated a fortune of £90,000 in six years, who, single-handed, defied for two years the civil and military authorities in Bengal, and who ruined an ex-Governor by litigation, and revenged himself on the Company for his forcible deportation, first by publishing a bitter attack on their administration in Bengal, and afterwards by establishing rival factories in the East Indies under the protection of the Imperial Austrian Government. Though his name is now almost forgotten, a sketch of his career may prove of interest, owing to the incidental light which it throws on the social conditions of the time and on the relations of the Company's servants with the natives of Bengal and with rival European traders.

Willem Bolts was a Dutchman by birth, although he afterwards posed as a vindicator of the rights of Englishmen against oppression and tyranny in high places. He was born in Holland in 1735, and came to England about the year 1749, where he appears to have served a commercial apprenticeship in a merchant's office. Thence he proceeded, some four or five years later, to Lisbon,[1] where he was an eye-witness of the great earthquake of 1755, and is said to have lost thereby all that he possessed.

---

[1] Probably to an English house of business there ; see page 139.

In the year 1759, he tells us, he

"petitioned the East India Company, in the usual mode, to be admitted into their service: on which the Court of Directors were pleased to appoint him a factor, with nine other gentlemen, on the Bengal establishment."

An original appointment as Factor was unusual; civilians generally commenced their service on the lowest rung of the ladder as writers, at the age of fifteen or sixteen, whereas Mr Bolts was five-and-twenty years of age when he landed in India. The exceptional step taken by the Directors on this occasion was due partly to the disorganisation of the Bengal service and the depletion of the cadre consequent on the capture and recapture of Calcutta in 1756 and 1757, and the loss of so many gallant civilian volunteers, and partly to resignations. In a letter from the Court of Directors dated the 23rd of November 1759, it is stated that on account of numerous resignations

"we have thought it expedient to engage some persons well experienced in business in some measure to supply the defect, and have accordingly appointed them to be Factors to be ranked under our Presidency at Fort William."

Here follow the names of the ten candidates selected, " Mr Bolts " being the last on the list.

"And we do appoint them to take their station on the list next under Mr Thomas Trench, and that such their rank be constantly observed by their being at no time hereafter superseded by anyone who does now or shall stand below them without our express directions in that behalf."

The terms of this injunction certainly lend some colour of justice to the complaint made by Mr Bolts at a later period, that the promotion over his head of two civilians junior to him on the list was a violation on the part of the President and Council of his contract with the Company. By the covenants which he entered into with the Company in the year 1759 he agreed to serve them for a term of five years, and was "authorised to trade in any port or place within the limits of their charter, subject to existing or future regulations and restrictions."

William Bolts received his appointment in London in November 1759. He arrived in Bengal "in the summer of 1760,"[1] and, as he tells us, "applied himself wholly to the acquisition of the Bengal dialect," rarely studied by Englishmen at that period. Bengali, in fact, was universally neglected for

"the Hindostan, a dialect introduced with Mohammedanism, and which the superior natives, in their intercourses with the Moguls, their former, and the Europeans, their present masters, mostly affect to speak."

His intimate acquaintance with the language of the people of Bengal no doubt stood him in good stead in his commercial dealings with them and, added to his previous mercantile training,[2] gave him an initial advantage over all his civilian trade rivals which his natural shrewdness and business capacity did not fail to improve upon. He was, moreover, entirely un-embarrassed by any scruples in his methods of trad-ing and had no hesitation in employing all the authority and prestige of the Company and of the name of Englishman, which Clive's victory at Plassey had re-established on a firmer basis, in furtherance of his own private ends. Thus "in a short time after his arrival" he was able to enter into a partnership "on equal terms" with two members of Council, Mr John Johnstone and Mr William Hay, and in Calcutta he soon became the acting partner. The

[1] According to a note on page 3 of Verelst's "Bengal," a date which agrees with the statement recorded by Mr Bolts on page 9 of his "Considerations on India Affairs," Part II.

[2] "Regularly bred to business, almost from his childhood, in a merchant's accompting-house" is his own expression. "A full-grown mercantile monster, aged twenty-five," says an anonymous contemporary pamphleteer.

chief articles of commerce in which he dealt were woollens and other British staples, purchased at the Company's auctions in Calcutta, saltpetre, opium, cotton, imported down the Jumna, and diamonds, imported specially " by a new channel of his own from Panna and Chudderpoor."

As early as November 1761 we find Mr Bolts in a position to engage in extensive speculations in land, as he joins with five others in an offer to the Council to farm the "Corryjury lands,"[1] to clear a tract of 20,000 bighas[2] for tillage, and to pay for seven years a rent of Rs. 2,000 annually in addition to the salt duty. They undertake to pay a fine of 12 annas a bigha for every bigha short of the stipulated extent of land. For the next seven years they offer to clear 30,000 bighas and to pay a rent of Rs. 4,000, with a forfeit of 8 annas a bigha for failure to clear the stipulated amount; for the next seven years 35,000 bighas at a rent of Rs. 10,000. They reserve to themselves an option to throw up their contract at the end of any term of seven years. How profitable were the terms on which the enterprising trio sometimes succeeded in obtaining land may be judged from a report written by Mr Verelst as Supervisor of Burdwan on the 14th of September 1765, and laid before the Select Committee.[3] He observes that he has been surprised to find the province subjected to a second "outcry," considering the losses caused by the first; that there was a general unwillingness to bid; that most of the few farms that had been let were let much below the former rent, but that there was an exception in the case of the farms lately held by Messrs Johnstone, Hay, and Bolts, on which a great advance was bid. In April 1767 the Select Committee reported that few

---

[1] Lands exempt from rent, or of which the revenue has been assigned to individuals or communities.
[2] A variable measure, usually about a third of an acre.
[3] See note page 21.

or no bidders appeared at the sale of farms held by Messrs Johnstone, Hay, and Bolts that they might not incur Mr Johnstone's displeasure, it being known that he intended them for himself. The peculiar methods of pushing their wares employed by Mr Bolts and his associates[1] soon brought them into conflict with the native authorities, and caused them to incur the censure of the President and subsequently of the Court of Directors. In October 1762 they had the temerity to address a letter direct to " Meer Sheer Aly Cham," Nawab of Purnea. It was couched in very rude terms, and protested against obstruction offered to the business of their agent Ram Charan Das. They accused him of having issued a proclamation boycotting those who traded with the English, stigmatised his conduct as a breach of the Emperor's firman, and threatened him with a complaint to the Nawab Mir Kasim, to be followed by exaction of reparation for all loss caused or about to be caused by his conduct.

In reply to this communication the Nawab notifies to Messrs Johnstone, Hay, and Bolts that he has published a proclamation prohibiting trade with the English under pain of fine or other punishment, and explains the prohibition as due to the quarrels and large outstanding debts caused by the system of trade advances. He promises, however, to assist the English "gomastahs" in all their ready money purchases, and pleads the orders of Nawab Mir Kasim for the measures he has taken.

In December 1762 Vansittart met the Nawab Mir Kasim at Monghyr, in order to put an end to the trade disputes which had arisen between the Company's servants and the Country Government. Here a treaty of commerce was agreed upon by which a

---

[1] Evasion of the payment of the customary duties, and the system of barhja and khichawat, *i.e.* forcing native merchants and shopkeepers to take their goods at 30, 40, or 50 per cent. above the market price.

general custom duty of 9 per cent. was imposed upon the inland trade of Europeans. European traders were at the same time prohibited from making advances and restricted to ready money transactions, and were made amenable to the jurisdiction of the Native Magistrates in respect of any disputes arising from their commercial concerns. This treaty was generally regarded by the English in Bengal as a gratuitous and unwarrantable surrender of their rights, and a large majority of the Council indignantly refused to ratify it. Two diametrically opposed views were held with regard to the original firman in favour of the East India Company. The majority of the Council maintained that the firman conferred on the Company and its servants a right to trade in India in all articles everywhere free of duty. The minority, Vansittart and Warren Hastings, thought that the firman granted no right to the inland trade. Their view was that the firman gave the English exemption from duties in their foreign trade, but left them upon the same footing as the natives with respect to the inland trade; that is to say, that they had a right to engage in it on payment of the customary duties to the Nawab's officers. In the salt trade, for example, from its commencement in 1758, English traders had regularly paid a duty of $2\frac{1}{2}$ per cent. on the price fixed in the Nawab's pass, equivalent to an "ad valorem" duty of about $4\frac{1}{2}$ per cent.[1] Even this was far below the duties paid by native merchants, which Mir Kasim estimated at 9 per cent., but which Vansittart found on enquiry to amount at several places up the river to 25 per cent. and upwards. It is significant that Lord Clive,

[1] Salt was at this period extraordinarily cheap. From a curious application to the Board, made in August 1764 by Mr Bolts as Secretary to the Committee of Lands, it appears that no less than 3 maunds, or 240 lbs., were then sold for one rupee.

as well as Warren Hastings, entertained the same opinion with regard to the inland trade. In his speech before the House of Commons on the 30th of March 1772, Lord Clive observed:

"Many years ago an expensive embassy was sent to Delhi to obtain certain grants and privileges from the Great Mogul in favour of the East India Company, and amongst others was obtained the privilege of trading duty free. The servants were indulged with this privilege, under the sanction of the Company's name. The Company never carried on any inland trade. Their Commerce has been confined to exports and imports only. It is impossible that the servants should have a more extensive right than the Company itself ever had. Yet they claimed a privilege of carrying on an inland trade duty free. The absurdity of a privilege so ruinous to the natives, and so prejudicial to the revenues of the country, is obvious. At the Revolution in 1757 no such claim was set up, nor was any such trade carried on publicly, or to my knowledge during my government, which ended in the beginning of the year 1760."

The views of the majority prevailing, however, Mr Amyatt[1] was deputed to visit Mir Kasim and urge the claim to an unrestricted inland trade custom free, while offering the Nawab, as an act of grace, a duty of $2\frac{1}{2}$ per cent. on salt only. The Nawab positively refused to subscribe to the revised articles; the dispute greatly widened the breach between him and the Bengal Government, and "was one of the real causes of the war" that soon followed, as Vansittart rightly contends.

[1] He never returned: he was assassinated by order of Mir Kasim.

CHAPTER II

GOVERNOR VANSITTART'S CAMPAIGN
AGAINST TRADE ABUSES

A N interesting correspondence laid before the
Council in January 1763 sets forth Vansittart's
honest, if not very judicious, endeavours to put a stop
to the oppression of the natives which the English
merchants and their "gomastahs," or trade agents,
practised, the obstructive tactics of some members of
the Council, the indignation of the European traders,
and the insolent attitude assumed towards the latter by
the native magistrates in some outlying places. With
a laudable desire to meet the complaints of Mir Kasim,
so far as they were well founded, Vansittart had
commissioned one Gungaram Mehter to enquire into
the alleged abuses and to put a stop to them where
he could. To anyone acquainted with the native
character the tactlessness of such a method and the
certain friction which must be engendered thereby
should have been sufficiently apparent. The gist
of the original "perwanah" [1] is as follows: "Mr
Vansittart is aware of the oppressive dealings of the
English 'gomastahs,' who stop and embargo goods
and force people to pay, thereby obliging the inhabitants to fly the country, and greatly prejudicing the
King's revenues. He orders Gungaram Mehter to
stop these oppressions, if he can, with a force of
'burkundazes'; [2] if not, he must enquire fully into

---

[1] Written authority or commission.
[2] Armed retainers or policemen.

them and report; whereupon the President and
Council will punish the wrongdoers." The report
of their agent, Ram Charan Das, on which Messrs
Johnstone, Hay, and Bolts based their remonstrance
to the Nawab of Purnea, describes a conversation with
the latter, who objected to his giving trade advances
and refused to assist him in recovering them. The
Nawab declared that he had received an explicit order
from "Nabob Kossim Ally Khan," that the English
"gomastahs" should only be allowed to make ready
money purchases. Ram Charan further asserted that
at "Sookasol" timber merchants had received orders
not to sell timber to the English, and that the Nawab
had laid a prohibitive duty on any such sale. Writing
from Goalpara in the Assam Valley on the 10th of
November 1762, a Mr Robinson complains of the
insolent attitude of the natives, and protests against
the authorisation of such a person as "Gungaram
Metre" to act as an inquisitor into the proceedings
of the English "gomastahs." The correspondence
includes a translation of a letter from Gungaram to
a Mr Teixira, demanding that he and his friends
should cease from their "oppressive proceedings";
a translation of a letter from the "Phouzdar[1] of
Rangamutty," to Mr Robinson, expressed in insolent
language, in which he admits having stopped Mr
Robinson's boats, declares that it was his duty to the
King to do so, in order to protect the royal revenues
from loss, accuses him of wishing to injure the revenues,
and demands to be shown a perwanah authorising Mr
Robinson's proceedings; and a translation of the orders
of "Nabob Cossim Ally Kawn" to the Faujdar
prohibiting trade advances from English "gomastahs"
to the ryots. On receipt of this correspondence,
accompanying a complaint from Messrs Johnstone,
Hay, and Bolts, the Governor addressed a letter to

[1] Magistrate.

these gentlemen in which he observes that he has himself always paid the customary duties on his private trade and requires others to do the same, asks for a list of the alleged duties demanded by the Faujdar of Rangamati; and emphasises the illegality of the methods of compulsion and intimidation resorted to by some European traders, "especially those of the Dacca gentlemen." He explains his orders to Gungaram Mehter, but admits that the latter may have exceeded his instructions, and adds that he has ordered him to return and report what he has seen and heard. At the same time the President addressed a vigorous complaint of Mr Bolts's conduct to the Council. In their rejoinder, dated the 14th of January 1763, Messrs Johnstone, Hay, and Bolts repudiate the President's insinuation, "casting a sidelong slur upon them," that the writing of the notorious letter to the Nawab of Purnea was the separate act of Mr Bolts, and assume joint responsibility for it. They defend the issue of the letter, and say that "Sheer Allee Cawn's" answer—admitting that "the Nabob" has ordered trade to be confined to ready money purchases—sufficiently vindicates the necessity of writing it. They accuse the President, Mr Vansittart, of unwillingness to believe complaints made by Englishmen against the Country Powers, and deny that their "gomastahs" ever lent money out at interest as "Sheer Allee Cawn" insinuates. They complain bitterly of the indignity offered to themselves, to the Council, and to all English gentlemen, of the insolent proceedings of the President's "black inquisitor, Gungaram Metre," as narrated by Mr Robinson, and of the failure of the Governor to redress their grievances against the Faujdar of Rangamati. These complaints found a ready echo in the Council, the members of which were personally interested in the removal of restrictions from their private trading ventures, Messrs Watts, Johnstone, and Hay especially distinguishing themselves by the bitterness of their invectives against the President.[1] It is interesting to note that the only supporter in Council of the President's honourable endeavour to secure justice for the raiats and native merchants was Warren Hastings. He both spoke and voted against the views of the majority of the Board, who recorded the following resolution on the whole correspondence at their meeting of the 17th of January: "The Board are of opinion that these documents sufficiently account for and vindicate these gentlemen" [Messrs Johnstone, Hay, and Bolts] "in that transaction." With regard to the Governor's letter of the 10th of January to Nawab Mir Kasim, in which he laid down regulations for private trade, they placed on record their opinion that he had "assumed a right to which he was no ways authorised," and that his proposed regulations "were dishonourable to them as Englishmen, and tended to the ruin of all public and private trade." These resolutions had been passed in the absence of Vansittart, who at the next meeting of the Board recorded a minute in which he expressed his surprise and indignation at the proceedings of the previous meeting. He challenged the other members of the majority to prove the allegations made in their resolution on his letter to the Nawab. He thinks that the honour and dignity of Englishmen

"would be better maintained by a scrupulous and a careful restraint of the 'dustucks'[2] . . . and by putting our gomastahs under some

---

[1] The dismissal, by order of the Directors, of three of his supporters in the Council, Messrs Pleydell, Sumner, and McGuire, had given Mr Vansittart's opponents a majority. The hostility to him was due partly to the jealousy and ill-feeling of those members whose promotion had been barred by the transfer of Mr Vansittart from Madras to the office of President, partly to dislike of his policy of compromise with the Nawab.

[2] Free passes for goods.

checks, than by suffering them to exercise an authority in the country, everyone according to the means put into his hands, and by their bringing an odium upon the name of the English by repeated violences done to the inhabitants."

As to Messrs Johnstone, Hay, and Bolts, he remarks that "every step he can take for the redress of the inhabitants is complained of as an encroachment upon the privileges of the English," and he appeals to the Directors against the Council's endorsement of their injurious accusations against him.

CHAPTER III

THE OPPRESSION OF THE ENGLISH GOMASTAHS

WHAT the titular ruler of Bengal thought of the proceedings of the English "gomastahs" may be judged from his letter to the Governor written in May 1762, in which he complains:

"And this is the way your Gentlemen behave; they make a disturbance all over my country, plunder the people, injure and disgrace my servants. . . . In every pergunnah and every village they have established ten or twenty new factories, and setting up the colours and showing the dustucks of the Company, they use their utmost endeavours to oppress the reiats, merchants, and other people of the country. The dustucks[1] for searching the boats which you formerly favoured me with, . . . the Englishmen by no means regard, but bring shame and disgrace upon my people, holding themselves in readiness to beat and abuse them. Having established these new factories, they carry on such business as the Company never heard of; and every Bengal gomastah makes a disturbance at every factory, and thinks himself not inferior to the Company. In every pergunnah, every village, and every factory, they buy and sell salt, beetle-nut, rice, straw, bamboos, fish, gunnies, ginger, sugar, tobacco, opium, and many other things. . . . They forcibly take away the goods and commodities of the reiats, merchants, etc., for a fourth part of their value; and by ways of violence and oppressions, they oblige the reiats to give five rupees for goods which are worth but one rupee; and for the sake of five rupees they bind and disgrace an Assammee,[2] who pays one hundred rupees malguzaree;[3] and they allow not any authority to my servants. Near four or five hundred new factories have been established in my dominions; and it is impossible to express what disturbances are made in every factory, and how the inhabitants are oppressed. The

---

[1] Warrants.   [2] A person on whom a claim is made.   [3] Land-tax.

officers of every district have desisted from the exercise of their functions; so that by means of these oppressions, and my being deprived of my duties, I suffer a yearly loss of near twenty-five lacks of rupees.[1] . . . Every one of these gomastahs has such a power, that he imprisons the collector, and deprives him of all authority whenever he pleases."

Lest this formidable indictment should be thought to have been inspired wholly by the prejudice of one whose interests were materially affected, the testimony of civilian witnesses may be cited in corroboration of the Nawab's plaint. In his "Narrative of the Transactions in Bengal," Vansittart quotes from letters addressed to the Governor by Mr George Gray, Chief at Malda, and Mr Senior, Chief at "Cossimbuzar." The former writes early in 1764:

"Since my arrival here, I have had an opportunity of seeing the villainous practices used by the Calcutta gomastahs in carrying on their business. The Government have certainly too much reason to complain of their want of influence in their country, which is torn to pieces by a set of rascals, who in Calcutta walk about in rags, but when they are sent out on gomastahships, lord it over the country, imprisoning the reiats and merchants, and talking in the most insolent, domineering manner to the fougedars and officers."

The latter observes:

"It would amaze you, the number of complaints that daily come before me, of the extravagances committed by our agents and gomastahs all over the country."

Mr Vansittart adds:

"I could produce many other proofs from the Company's records of the reality of the oppression the country people suffer from the English agents and gomastahs employed in the inland trade. . . . The Nabob Meer Jaffier[2] complains of it as much since his re-establishment, as he did in his first administration. In short he repeatedly complained to the Governor and Council . . . that it was impossible for his Government to subsist upon such a footing, and earnestly pressed for the abolition of it, notwithstanding the consent he was obliged to give in his treaty of July 1763."

---

[1] Over a quarter of a million sterling.
[2] Who was reinstated after the defeat of Mir Kasim at Buxar.

Two years earlier similar testimony had been borne by Warren Hastings in a letter which he addressed to Governor Vansittart, dated " Bauglepoor " April 25, 1762.

"I beg leave to lay before you a grievance, which loudly calls for redress, and will, unless duly attended to, render ineffectual any endeavours to create a firm and lasting harmony between the Nabob and the Company.   I mean the oppressions committed under the sanction of the English name, and through the want of spirit in the Nabob's subjects to oppose them.   This evil, I am well assured, is not confined to our dependents alone, but is practised all over the country, by people falsely assuming the habits of our seepoys, or calling themselves our gomastahs.   As on such occasions the great power of the English intimidates the people from making any resistance ; so, on the other hand, the indolence of the Bengalees, or the difficulty of gaining access to those who might do them justice, prevents our having knowledge of their oppressions, and encourages their continuance, to the great, though unmerited scandal of our government.   I have been surprised to meet with several English flags flying in places which I have passed ; and on the river I do not believe I passed a boat without one.   By whatever title they have been assumed (for I could only trust to the information of my eyes, without stopping to ask questions) I am sure their frequency can bode no good to the Nabob's revenues, the quiet of the country, or the honour of our nation, but evidently tends to lessen each of them.

A party of seepoys, who were on the march before us, afforded sufficient proofs of the rapacious and insolent spirit of those people, where they are left to their own discretion.   Many complaints of them were made me on the road ; and most of the petty towns and serais were deserted at our approach, and the shops shut up, from the apprehension of the same treatment from us.

You are sensible, Sir, that it is from such little irregularities, too trivial perhaps for public complaint, and continually repeated, that the country people are habituated to entertain the most unfavourable notions of our government ; and by them the English credit suffers much more than by matters which are made of greater consequence in the debates between the Nabob and us."

In March 1763 Messrs Johnstone, Hay, and Bolts return to the charge with a complaint to the Council of the insolent behaviour of a Zilladar [1] who has con-

---

[1] District Officer.

fiscated salt for which their agent had given advances, and fined and imprisoned several raïats on their farm, and rudely refused redress. They demand that the Zilladar should be summoned to appear before the Council. In August of the same year Mr William Bolts applies to the President and Council in behalf of the Committee of Lands, acquainting them that there is a balance of Rs. 9,700 due from Mr Samuel Griffiths on his farm for the year 1761, which cannot be recovered, after frequent applications to his attorney, and asks them to take measures for the recovery of the Committee's balance.

When the Directors at length pronounced judgment, they completely vindicated Mr Vansittart from the aspersions cast upon him by the majority of his Council, and censured the civilian firm of traders in the following terms :

" The conduct and behaviour of Mr William Bolts, a factor, falling next under our consideration, they appear, so far as he was connected with Messrs Johnstone and Hay, to be very improper; especially in joining with them in an audacious and impertinent letter to the Fouzdar of Purnea, as it stands on your consultations of the 27th December 1762, and for which the President recommended it to the Council to pass some censure upon him. He appears likewise to have been guilty of irregular practices in respect of the carrying on his private trade : let him be called into council, and reprimanded according to his deserts ; and inform him, if his conduct is not more satisfactory for the future, we shall dismiss him from the service."

On receipt of this censure, in July 1764, Mr Bolts writes to the President and Council, expressing his sorrow at the displeasure of the Directors. He replies to the accusation of irregular practices that he has been guilty of no dishonesty ; he attributes their censure to imperfect information as to the facts, or to the wilful misrepresentation of others ; he winds up with a demand for an enquiry, in order to clear him of the charges made against him.

CHAPTER IV

MESSRS JOHNSTONE, HAY, AND BOLTS'S
AGENT VINDICATED

MEANWHILE, earlier in 1764, Mr Bolts had been appointed second in Council at the factory at Benares, at which Mr Randolph Marriott was chief. He had by this time become the head of a large business, and had accumulated a very considerable private fortune. His undoubted capacity had been previously recognised officially by his appointment as President of the Court of Cutcherry ;[1] writing in May 1763, he complains that he cannot get a quorum of the Court to sit, though it has nine members besides himself, and asks to be allowed to sit *sole*, in default of any other remedy for the non-attendance of the members.

On the 11th of February 1764, the marriage of "William Bolts, Esq., and Ann Aston, Spinster," of Calcutta, was celebrated in St John's Chapel, which stood in the ruins of the old Fort, and con-

---

[1] Writing in 1764, the anonymous author of "A Vindication of Mr Holwell's Character" gives an account of this court. The Zemindarry, or Court of Cutcherry, was "a tribunal constituted for the hearing, trying, and determining all matters and things, both civil and criminal, wherein the natives only, subjects of the Mogul, are concerned. He (the Zemindar) tried in a summary way, had the power of lash, fine, and imprisonment ; he determined all matters of meum and tuum ; and in all criminal cases, proceeded to sentence and punishment, immediately after hearing. . . . He has also the power to condemn thieves, and other culprits, to work in chains upon the roads, during any determinate space of time, or for life. In all causes of property, an appeal lay to the President and Council against his decrees." He adds that, at the recommendation of Mr Holwell, the Court of Directors in the year 1758 changed the constitution of the court, appointing three judges, members of the Board, in monthly rotation, instead of one.

tinued to be used as the Presidency Church till 1787, when the present St John's Church was consecrated. The bride must have been very many years younger than her husband ; indeed, if the statement made in the certificate of her death at Chandermagore in 1821 were correct, she would have been only twelve years old, for her age at death is given as sixty-nine years. Probably she was at least two or three years older than that when she died.

The Council were kept pretty busy with the affairs of Messrs Johnstone, Hay, and Bolts throughout the year 1764. On the representation of Mr Jekyll, Resident at Rangpur, the Board had issued an order recalling the firm's agent at Dinajpur, Mr Philip Pollock. On the 9th day of May they acknowledge the receipt of the Board's orders, which, they remark, had been long anticipated,

" for the oppressive proceedings of the Company's Agents in those parts for their own private interests, particularly Mr Jekyll's, have long since obliged them to recall him, and he has been five weeks in Calcutta."

They regret that they were not consulted as to the truth of the charges made against their agent before his recall was ordered ; they are ignorant of the charges against Mr Pollock, and are therefore unable at present to refute them ; they have always found him strictly upright, and popular with the natives, and quote a testimonial to this effect from the Nawab. The question is, not " Does Mr Pollock oppress the ryotts ? " but " Does Mr Pollock or others dare attempt to purchase goods of free trade in opposition to Mr Jekyll ? " The complaints are not made spontaneously, but hunted up by Mr Jekyll to enable him to extort contracts for his own private account. They have long been suffering from the tyranny of Mr Jekyll, and have made frequent applications to him for redress of their grievances without being vouchsafed any reply. They continue, quite in the best manner of Junius : "When injustice is armed with power and determined on oppression, the strongest pleas of innocence are preferred in vain." They request that Mr Jekyll may not be allowed to be his own judge, and that orders may be issued to put a stop to his irregularities. If their complaints are found to be just, they urge that Mr Pollock, if he is sent back to Dinajpur, may be put on the same footing as other agents. Their complaint is accompanied by numerous letters instancing acts of violence and oppression committed by Mr Jekyll's orders. The gist of all these is, that the raiats had accepted advances from Messrs Johnstone, Hay, and Bolts, for opium and other commodities, whereupon Mohun Shaw, Mr Jekyll's agent, seized and imprisoned them for refusing to repudiate their existing contracts and to accept "dadney"[1] from him instead. Their agent, Durgaram Das, alleges that Mohun Shaw had a " perwanah " from Mr Jekyll.

Having considered these documents, the Select Committee,[2] at their meeting of the 17th May 1764, recorded the following resolution :

"Agreed we write to Cossimbuzar with a copy of them desiring the gentlemen there to transmit the same to Mr Jekyll, with directions to send the gomastah Mohun Shaw down to Calcutta immediately; and as we observe particularly that Messrs Johnstone, Hay, and Bolts complain of their having by themselves and their agent, Mr Pollock, represented their grievances to Mr Jekyll without receiving any answer, and in their letter No. 5 that this Mohun Shaw appears to have acted from the authority of a perwannah of Mr Jekyll's, that we desire Mr Jekyll may give us an immediate answer to the truth of these circumstances." "Ordered that Messrs Johnstone, Hay, and Bolts be advised in answer of our having sent these orders, and directed to deliver to the President

---

[1] Advances made to craftsmen or cultivators by traders.

[2] A kind of Cabinet, or inner ring, of the Council, usually consisting of three or four members. For a general view of its functions and limitations, see pages 105 and 106.

a list of the pykars [1] on whose evidence they mean to rest the proofs of their accusation against Mohun Shaw, that a letter may be sent to the Phousdar to have them sent down."

Mr Jekyll's defence was read at a meeting of the Council held on the 9th of July. It was not considered satisfactory, for he was ordered

"to give an immediate reply to the question, which he has evaded answering, did he grant the perwannah mentioned in Durgaram Dass's letter No. 5, on the authority of which Mohun Shaw seems to have acted?"

At a previous meeting, held on the 3rd of July, a letter had been received from Messrs Johnstone, Hay, and Bolts, in which they announced that their witnesses were all in Calcutta, but that Mohun Shaw was being detained by Mr Jekyll for the purpose of extorting false declarations from raiats and others, and they sent a specimen, a written statement extorted from their own gomastah, " Rangopaul," denying that he had been obstructed in his business or had told his master so.

On the 25th of July Messrs Johnstone and Co.'s witnesses were examined before the Board, and on the following day it was agreed

"to acquaint Mr Jekyll with the proceedings and to tell him that the charge of confining and beating some of the pycars with an intention to force them to contract for saltpetre being clearly proved, we shall keep Mohun Shaw in confinement and determine further how he shall be punished when we receive Mr Jekyll's answer . . . whether he issued the perwannah to Mohun Shaw. . . . What was the nature of that perwannah, and, in general; how far he authorised these proceedings . . ., etc., and calling for Mr Jekyll's judicial diary."

It was not till the 24th of November following that final orders were passed, when Mr Bolts and his friends came off with flying colours:

"A motion being made that the Board should come to a determination on the subject of the accusation against Mohun Shaw, the gomastah of Mr Jekyll, Resident at Rungpore. . . . It appears to the Board that Mohun Shaw did exceed the orders of

---

[1] Brokers, retail-dealers.

his master and gave unlawful interruption to the business of Messrs Johnstone, Hay, and Bolts, and other gentlemen, and they therefore think him deserving of punishment; but esteeming the long confinement he has suffered to be sufficient . . . it is ordered that he be released. At the same time the Board think it necessary in order to obviate any reflections that may be cast to the prejudice of the gentlemen concerned in that trade, to give it as their opinion that in carrying it on they did not give any interruption to the Company's business."

The partisans of free inland trade were now completely in the ascendant.

In February 1765 Mir Jafir died, and his eldest surviving son, Nujum-ud-Daula, was recognised as Nawab of Bengal. Spencer, an importation from Bombay, had succeeded Vansittart as President in the previous December; he and his Council renewed with Mir Jafir's son the clause inserted in the last treaty with his father, by which the inland trade was to be open free of all duties, except a 2½ per cent duty on salt, to the servants of the Company. This was an act of flagrant disobedience to the Directors' orders of the 8th of February and the 1st of June 1764 for the discontinuance of the inland trade. All the members of Council accepted unconscionable presents from the new Nawab and from his newly appointed chief minister, Muhammad Riza Ali Khan. In the general scramble for wealth which then ensued no one distinguished himself so much as Mr Bolts's partner, Mr John Johnstone. This gentleman had been much shocked when Vansittart and his colleagues were the recipients of Mir Kasim's generosity, and had strenuously upheld the principle that all such presents should be placed to the credit of the Company. On the present occasion he headed the list of "commissions" by receiving a sum of two lakhs and 37,000 rupees for himself, and 50,000 for his brother, Mr Gideon Johnstone, who was not even in the Company's service.

CHAPTER V

THE UNSCRUPULOUSNESS OF MR BOLTS

THE year 1765 found Mr Bolts involved in two shady transactions, both of which illustrate his thorough unscrupulousness.

In that year all civil servants were required by order of the Directors to sign a formal agreement, in which they had to subscribe to the prohibition against accepting any presents from native princes in India. The Government of Bengal had changed hands in May 1765, Lord Clive having superseded Mr Spencer as Governor. Assisted by Messrs Sumner, Sykes, and Verelst, and General Carnac, as members of a Select Committee temporarily vested by the Directors with extraordinary powers, until peace and tranquillity should be restored in Bengal, Clive was carrying matters with a high hand for the reform of abuses, and riding rough-shod over the prejudices of members of the Board like Messrs Johnstone and Leicester, men who were traders first and civilians afterwards. Long before the arrival of Clive the covenants had reached Bengal; but Spencer and his Council were too busy arranging for and receiving presents from the new Nawab to pay any attention to the Directors' orders. Indeed it is not surprising to read that they disapproved of the prohibition on principle, and that Mr Johnstone memorialised the Directors on the subject. The Select Committee, however, now ordered the immediate execution of the covenants. There was great unwillingness on the part of many civilians to submit to the Directors' prohibition, and Mr Bolts endeavoured in characteristically impudent fashion to evade it. His covenant was signed on or about the 9th May 1765; but instead of subscribing it himself, he employed a writer to sign his name for him.[1] Later on, having become aware that Mr Edward Baber, Assistant-Secretary to the Board, had discovered the trick, he became uneasy, and formed the bold design of procuring the withdrawal of the genuine covenant with the spurious signature and substituting a spurious covenant with a genuine signature. From a deposition obtained from Mr Baber, it appears that in September 1766 Mr Bolts asked Mr Baber to be allowed to see his contract. When the request was granted, in a private room by Mr Bolts's desire, he pressed the Assistant-Secretary for a long time to let him execute the covenant afresh, and take it to his own house for the purpose, giving as his reason that Mr Isaac Sage, who had succeeded Mr Marriott as Chief at Benares, was aware that the signature to the covenant was not in Mr Bolts's handwriting, but in that of his writer, and that Mr Sage might use the knowledge to his detriment. Mr Baber refused. Mr Bolts renewed his solicitation, and Mr Baber proposed to consult a Mr Campbell, a friend of Mr Bolts, a proposal which the latter gentleman rejected. Mr Bolts finally asked Mr Baber to keep this matter a profound secret, which the latter agreed to do only as long as he should judge it to be consistent with his duty to the Company. This interesting deposition is printed in full in the appendix to Verelst's " Bengal."[2]

[1] See Counsel's opinion on this transaction, quoted in the Directors' letter of March 1770, at pages 103 and 104.
[2] Mr Bolts subsequently prosecuted Mr Baber, possibly for libel on account of this deposition. See page 103.

BOLTS v. MARRIOTT

The other episode of the same year, in which Mr Bolts played a discreditable part, throws a strong light upon the prevalent corruption of the time. Having discovered that Mr Marriott, his senior in command at Benares, was making a large profit out of the Mint, he quarrelled with him on account of his refusal to share his illegitimate gains with his junior, and reported Mr Marriott's conduct to the Board. Mr Marriott had entered into a joint venture with Major Munro to farm the Mint at Benares; they paid to the Government at Delhi an annual rent of Rs. 30,000 a year, the revenue being at that time estimated at Rs. 50,000. An acrimonious correspondence commenced in August 1765 between Messrs Marriott and Bolts on this and other matters, particularly an alleged illegal confinement of a native merchant, named "Sadallo," and continued until February of the following year. The whole correspondence was laid before the Board at their meeting of the 17th of February 1766, and the Board then proceeded to an examination of the parties, as follows :

EXAMINATION OF MR BOLTS

Q. "When you confined the merchant, whether was it by seapoys or the Government's people?

A. Neither one nor the other, but by my own Peons under whose charge he was kept until such time as he could be delivered over to the Cutwal,[1] but how long that was I do not exactly recollect.

Q. Did you acquaint Mr Marriott with your having confined this man previous to your receiving Mr Marriott's first note?

A. No, for the reason mention'd in my address to the Board.

Q. At the time you demanded a share of the profit Mr Marriott

---

[1] Police officer, superintendent of police.

reaped from the Mint, did you know that it was the President and Council's orders that no Company's servants should enjoy any post or employment under the Government?

A. I did know that it was against orders, and have already spoke to this in my address to the Board on this subject, which was wrote a very few days after obtaining knowledge of Mr Marriott's being concerned in the Mint.

(Mr Marriott desires Mr Bolts may be asked how many days he means by ' a very few days.')

A. Within a month.

Q. Did you ever acquaint Mr Marriott with the complaints against his banyan [1] before the dispute happened between Mr Marriott and you?

A. I had several amicable conversations with Mr Marriott on the subject, and Mr Graham my predecessor had frequently even warm expostulations with him upon the same subject.

(Mr Bolts being asked by Mr Marriott what were the particular complaints, answers:)

A. They were touching Mr Marriott's ' banyans ' being entrusted with those transactions that were properly the department of the Council.

(Mr Marriott then asked if there was any particular abuse complained of.)

A. No; time did not admit of it, there being only four or five days between my leaving Mr Marriott's house and the breaking out of the dispute between us, and as I knew that disputes must unavoidably come, I delayed representing those grievances while I lived in Mr Marriott's house."

The Board desiring Mr Bolts to declare whether he ever knew it was a standing order that all applications to the Country Government should be made through the Chief,

He answers :

"I never understood this order in any other light than with regard to private correspondence with the Country Government, but that in every other matter I apprehended the Chief ought never to stir without the knowledge of his Council, conceiving the contrary tends only to render the Chief despotic, and his Council useless."

---

[1] Native secretaries or stewards.

EXAMINATION OF MR MARRIOTT

Q. " As it appears by the sunnad [1] that the Mint and Cutwallee [2] was given up to the Company by the King, had you any authority from the President and Council to surrender them up again to the King?

A. I had no such authority, but as it was a transaction of Major Munro's and mine, I imagined it had been represented to the Board, as he carried on all the correspondence at that time.

Q. Were the revenues arising from those two offices brought to the credit of the Company before giving them to the King?

A. No; for nothing was collected till after the treaty with Bulwant Sing [3] was signed by General Carnac and myself.

Q. What was the reason you did not make the publication Mr Bolts proposed regarding your banyan?

A. Because I never could get Mr Bolts to produce any particular charge against the banyan.

Q. When Mr Bolts desired a share in the profits of the Mint, did he desire it only conditionally in case those profits were authorised by the Board?

A. No; for if he had, I could not have had the least pretence for objection."

The Board having no further questions to ask, Mr Bolts desires leave to make the following remarks:

"That the declaration of Diaram Havildar is entirely false, and it is extraordinary that it never was exhibited at Benares. That Sadallo's petition applying for redress was wrote in Mr Marriott's chamber three days after the petitioner had received all the redress Mr Marriott could give him, which was rescuing him from the King's officers by a party of seapoys. And that the said petition was not made mention of by Mr Marriott to the Board."

The extract which follows shows that Mr Marriott consulted Lord Clive on the question whether the renting of the Mint from the King was a violation of his covenant with the Company. The President

---

[1] Deed of Grant.   [2] Police administration.
[3] A raja who held part of the province and subahship of Oudh, including Benares and the neighbouring territory, under the Nawab Shuja-u-Daula. His son Chait Singh came into conflict with Hastings.

observing that Mr Marriott in one of his letters in the
course of these proceedings makes a quotation from a
letter of his to his Lordship, produces the following
extract from his Lordship's answer :

EXTRACT FROM LORD CLIVE'S LETTER TO MR MARRIOTT

"NEAR BOGLIPORE
16th July 1765.

"The advice you ask of me concerning the covenants is of so
delicate and particular a nature that I cannot with any propriety
take upon me to give you my opinion, since anything I can say will
not have the least weight in a Court of Chancery.   Indeed all the
advice I can give you, is, to give the covenants a serious consideration and follow the dictates of your own conscience, for there
is nothing else that I know which can give the covenants any
weight."

From an entry in the "General Journal for 1763–
1764" it appears that Mr Marriott, in consulting Lord
Clive, sought rather an ex-post-facto vindication of
an accomplished fact than advice regarding a contemplated transaction.   The entry is :—"Advanced
Randolph Marriott, Esq., September 1763, Rs.
72,000."

DECISION OF THE BOARD

"The parties withdrawing, having no further remarks to make,
the Board reconsidered the whole proceedings and unanimously
Agreed that Mr Marriott is highly culpable in renting the Mint,
knowing it was against the orders of the Board for any servant of
the Company to enjoy any post or employment under the Country
Government, and therefore ought to bring to the Company's credit
all the profits that have accrued to him from the Mint—but they
humbly hope in consideration of Mr Marriott's general good
character that the Company will be satisfied with the money he
paid to the King, together with the advantages he has received
upon restamping his own specie, and take no further notice of the
affair.
    With regard to Mr Bolts they regard him as highly deserving of
censure for the disrespect he was guilty of towards his Chief in
taking upon himself to arrest Sadallo, and in which he was the

more culpable as it is very doubtful whether Coja Petruse,[1] in whose name he acted, had any right to sue for the bond in question. Nor do they allow him any merit in the discovery of the Mint, as there is reason to believe he was too much influenced thereto from his being refused a share therein by Mr Marriott."

The lenience of the judgment on Mr Marriott and the silence with regard to Major Munro are noticeable ; but the latter was in England during this year. Perhaps in consequence of the discredit which he had incurred in this affair, Mr Bolts was recalled from Benares in the autumn of 1765, and Mr Isaac Sage, his junior on the list, was appointed to succeed Mr Marriott as Chief. This appointment must have been sufficiently galling to a man of Mr Bolts's undoubted ability, especially as it appears to have been made in contravention of the Directors' orders of the 23rd of November 1759.

Mr Bolts and Lord Clive's Diamonds

In a despatch of the 4th of March 1769 the Directors acquiesced in the Board's order that Mr Marriott should refund all the profits he had made out of the Mint at Benares, and prohibited his promotion without their express consent. With regard to Mr Bolts they observed :

"We agree with you that the part Mr Bolts has acted at Benares as represented in your letter is highly deserving of censure, and if his conduct in future is not perfectly to your satisfaction, we recommend it to you to suspend or dismiss him the service, as you shall judge his behaviour may deserve."

Before he quitted Benares, he made an attempt to secure no less a personage than Lord Clive as his partner in a speculation in diamonds. In his "Con-

---

[1] Coja Petruse was one of the two Armenian ministers of the revolution which raised Mir Kasim to the throne. Writing in 1764, Sir Eyre Coote says that he "resides in Calcutta, retained by Cossim Aly Chan, a known spy upon every transaction of the English, of which he never fails to give his master the most regular intelligence."

siderations " he tells the story of his connection with Lord Clive in such a manner as to convey the imputation of bad faith and commercial greed to the latter. It is to be observed, however, that he is unable to adduce any proof of his allegation that Lord Clive had originally accepted his proposal; nor does he produce the letter of the 4th of October 1765, in which Lord Clive is alleged to have withdrawn from his previous verbal agreement. The passage runs as follows :

"When Lord Clive was at Banáras in the beginning of August 1765, the writer communicated to him the plan he had formed for the bringing of diamonds direct from the mines, to which he had already sent an agent. His Lordship approved of the scheme and verbally agreed to take a concern in it; but soon afterwards so far altered his mind as to quit his engagement and undertake the engrossing of it himself; for which purpose he established Mr John Chamier as his agent at Banáras."

(It is worthy of remark that Mr Bolts's quarrel with Mr Marriott began in August 1765, and that Lord Clive, who must have become acquainted by the month of October with a sufficient amount of the Bolts and Marriott correspondence to give him a pretty accurate idea of Mr Bolts's character, would naturally be chary of committing himself to any association with that unscrupulous adventurer.)

"By a letter dated the 4th October his Lordship informed the writer that he had given over all thoughts of purchasing diamonds; but at the time that letter came to hand, the writer was shewn, by Mr Chamier, other letters from his Lordship, in which he had given that gentleman, as his agent, orders to make very large purchases of them, while at the same time he cautioned him to be aware of Bolts. This was sufficient information to the writer of what he had to expect. Dissembling, however, his real sentiments on the noble Lord's giving up his intended share, the writer kept on his own account the parcels purchased by the agent first employed, and relinquished the trade ; which his Lordship, by his own agent, then engaged in, with the assistance of the very servants whom the writer had employed, and by the track of correspondence that he had opened."

The reply of Mr Bolts, to which he alludes above, was dated the 29th of October 1765, and was addressed to Mr Henry Strachey, Lord Clive's Secretary:

"I was duly favoured with your letter of the 2nd instant, as also one from his Lordship, dated the 4th.

As his Lordship has given over all thoughts of investing his money in diamonds, I also have entirely set aside that scheme, for my sole motive in that undertaking would have been to make myself serviceable to him.[1] I myself should not have bought a single stone, nor have offered to take a small concern, only his Lordship, in his conversation with me, told me he thought it would be best for me to hold a small share.   The trifle I have purchased, I shall have the pleasure of shewing to his Lordship in Calcutta.

In consequence of the orders of the Board, as soon as I get a budgerow,[2] which I am in daily expectation of, I shall set off for Calcutta."

That Lord Clive did make extensive purchases of diamonds is well known, and he explained the reason in a speech which he made in the House of Commons on the 30th of March 1772.   Speaking of the necessity of finding a mode of remitting the proceeds of his jaghir[3] (about Rs. 30,000 a year), he said: "For this purpose and this only, I sent an agent into a distant and independent country to make purchase of diamonds."   Taking all the circumstances into consideration, and allowing for the strong motive for misrepresentation which Mr Bolts had in his forcible seizure and deportation, it seems reasonable to suppose that what really happened was that Lord Clive was desirous of purchasing diamonds solely for the purpose of remittance, a very common practice in those days, and that he intended at first to employ Mr Bolts as his agent, but changed his mind on learning his real character.

[1] This, if Mr Bolts's account is assumed to be true, would be probable enough; he was at this time, no doubt, getting uneasy about the covenant signed by his writer, and would be glad of an ally so influential at the seat of Government.   [2] House-boat.
[3] Landed estate, granted by the Emperor for his military services.

CHAPTER VI

MR BOLTS SUSPENDED FROM THE
COMPANY'S SERVICE

VERY soon after Mr Bolts's removal from Benares, we find him petitioning the Board to be allowed to return. Writing on the 31st January 1766, he refers to the Board's orders to Mr Marriott and himself to repair to Calcutta, and deliver over "to the present provisional Resident" the charge of the factory during their absence. He asks their permission to return to his family at Benares. Should the factory be continued, he is perfectly satisfied with his present rank as Second; but in case the present establishment of Chief and Council be abolished and only a gentleman under Council be continued as President till the remainder of the Tunkah[1] money be recovered, he requests that he may be continued there in a public and not in a private capacity only, in order to settle his private concerns and bring his family down, an indulgence which he hopes will be esteemed his right from his rank and the rules of the service.

Mr Bolts's anxiety to return to the bosom of his family, though not unjustified by subsequent events, was probably a secondary consideration with him, his real motive for desiring to return being his extensive commercial concerns in that part of the Company's

---

[1] Tunkah, Hindustani "tankhwāh," is "an assignment on the revenue of a particular locality in favour of an individual" (Hobson-Jobson).

Thus the districts of Burdwan and Nuddea were assigned to the Company from April 1758 to April 1760 for the payment of Mir Jafir's debt incurred under the treaty of 1757.

territories. It is amusing to note his description of Mr Isaac Sage, Mr Marriott's successor at Benares, as "the present provisional Resident," and to contrast the language of mock humility and resignation under the slur cast upon him by the promotion of his junior with the expressions which he subsequently used in his petition to the Directors:

"That he resigned on account of the confusion and injustice which prevailed after the appointment of the Select Committee, all gradation of rank and service being set at nought, and every preferment to every office being disposed of from faction, private interest, and party, without any regard to merit or service."

The Board at their meeting of the 24th of February permitted him to return to Benares in a private capacity only, in order to settle his affairs, and gave him till the 1st July following.

Having obtained the desired permission to return to Benares, Mr Bolts showed no disposition to regard the Board's limitation of his period of residence. On the 28th of July following, finding Mr Bolts still at Benares nearly a month after he should have returned to Calcutta, the Board issued the following orders :

"Mr Bolts having exceeded the time limited in Cons. the 24th February last, for his return to Calcutta from Benares:
Ordered that Mr Sage, the resident at the factory, be directed to inform him that the Board are displeased with the neglect he has shown to their orders; that he is therefore to send him down immediately; and that unless Mr Bolts arrives in Calcutta by the 28th August, he will stand dismissed the service."

A month later Mr Bolts explains his reasons for disobeying the Board's orders, and coolly asks permission to continue his residence at Benares :

CONSULTATIONS, 25TH AUGUST 1766

"Letter from the Resident at Benares, dated the 12th instant, read, acknowledging the receipt of our letter of the 28th ultimo, enclosing a letter from Mr Bolts in answer to our orders regarding him, acquainting us, that as he is not sensible it is in his power to comply with that part of our instructions which requires him to take care Mr Bolts does not exceed the time prescribed, he shall wait our further commands before he ventures to take any step in so delicate an affair.

Letter from Mr Bolts . . . setting forth his reasons for having staid at Benares beyond the time we limited him to, and requesting us to indulge him with a longer stay to settle his own and the affairs of his constituents, which he represents to be extremely intricate. Agreed we write in answer to Mr Sage, that we did not imagine him to be so little acquainted with the nature of our orders as to be in doubt how far it behoved him to put them into execution ; that notwithstanding what Mr Bolts alledges in his letter, we are well assured, that, instead of making it his business to settle his affairs at Benares, which was the sole reason for his being permitted to return thither, he entered into new concerns; that he is therefore to inform Mr Bolts that we are determined our orders shall not be trifled with, and that he is to consider himself as suspended from the Company's service from the 28th of this month, for not complying with our positive injunction for his return to Calcutta. However, in consideration of the plausible reasons which he now, for the first time, assigns, he is further to acquaint Mr Bolts, that, provided he arrives in Calcutta by the 10th October, his suspension will be taken off, and, if for this purpose, he does not leave Benares by the 1st October, he is to send him away by force."

CHAPTER VII

ELOPEMENT OF MRS BOLTS

IN the light of his subsequent conduct, the connivance of Mr Sage in Mr Bolts's continued
disregard of the Board's notice to quit must be
esteemed highly suspicious. For it was on some
date between the 12th and 26th of August that he
eloped with Mrs Bolts to Patna. On the latter date
Mr Bolts writes from Benares acquainting the Board
that Mr Sage, their Resident at Benares, had quitted
the factory and carried off his wife with him, that the
budgerow in which they went had been traced so far
that there was no hope of Mr Sage's returning soon
to take charge of the Company's affairs, and that he
had presumed to interfere so far as to send the
Company's treasure to Patna, and to order the sepoys down in consequence of their former orders.
He added that according to the accounts of Mr
Sage's sircar[1] there was a sum of Rs. 120,000 of the
Company's money lying there, which he intended
despatching to Patna. The effect of the latter
portion of this damning report against Mr Sage had
been to a great extent discounted by the President's
previous reception of a letter from Mr Sage stating
that his departure to Patna was due to a summons
to attend a Court Martial,[2] and that he proposed
returning to Benares with all possible expedition.

It was not until the 22nd of October that Mr Sage
submitted the explanation of his conduct which the

---

[1] Accountant.   [2] See note on page 37.

Board called upon him to furnish. His letter, though distinguished by a considerable amount of cool effrontery, does not bear the appearance of being the answer of an innocent man cruelly slandered both in his private and in his official capacity. He denies absolutely the charge of eloping with Mrs Bolts, and refers them to her for a confirmation of his denial. He rebuts the accusation of deserting his station by replying that the Judge Advocate summoned him to attend the General Court Martial at Patna.[1] The Company has suffered no detriment from the officiousness of Mr Bolts, as Mr Middleton has informed the Board that he had received the balance from Mr Sage, and he flatters himself that Mr Bolts's letters will make no impression to his disadvantage.

Mr Bolts's reply to Mr Sage's defence, dated the 10th of November, was considered by the Council at their meeting of the 24th of November. It contained his formal resignation of the Company's service, and was accompanied by a most remarkable account of her elopement written by Mrs Anne Bolts. Apparently the evidence of husband and wife was disbelieved by the Board, for not only was no censure recorded on Mr Sage's conduct, but that gentleman's promotion does not seem to have been in any way retarded, and we find him some years later in the influential and dignified position of Chief of the Company's factory at Patna.

Mr Bolts's letter and his wife's narrative are sufficiently interesting to merit quotation in full. The former runs :

"Your Secretary has conformably to your directions transmitted me a copy of Mr Isaac Sage's letter, wherein he endeavours to apologise for his conduct in some points by palliation and in others

---

[1] For the trial of the mutinous officers, the ringleader of whom was Sir Robert Fletcher, second in command to Clive.

by a flat denial of the truth.   And I am obliged to you for giving
me this opportunity of publicly detecting the falsehood.

In a letter of the 10th September I acquainted Mr Sage with the
steps which had been taken by me at Banáras on his abandoning
the factory, sending him at the same time copies of my letters to the
Board of the 26th August and 3rd September, that he might in time
justify himself to his employers.   It is obvious that the badness of
his case has somewhat retarded his answer.   The reason he alleges
for quitting the factory was never thought of till after his flight.   He
had declared to me and others some time before that on an application which had been made to him he had represented his evidence
at the Court Martial would be of no moment and was excused from
going.   Was the factory to be deserted by the sudden and secret
absconding of the Resident, and one lakh seventy thousand rupees
of the Company's money abandoned by him a fortnight without being authorised by his superiors, and without any steps for the
security of the Company's property?   The accompanying letter will
further explain this affair, and if the palliation was not so gross as
to render a further elucidation needless, a scrutiny into the proceedings of the Courts Martial would further expose it.   In a letter
dated the 10th September I informed the President that a lakh and
a quarter of the Company's money which I had despatched from
Banáras arrived safe, and that I had taken the Chief of Patna's
receipt for it.   I therefore presume that the balance which Mr Sage
mentions to have paid Mr Middleton was what was due after the
above-mentioned despatch is brought to account, and if as Mr Sage
expresses it, 'The Company has suffered no detriment from my
officiousness,' it is very lucky that I prevented the detriment which
might have accrued from a breach of trust, by a timely interposition,
to save their property which was exposed to many unforseen acci-
dents that might have befallen it from the licentiousness of un-
bridled sepoys deserted by their Chief.

The other part of Mr Sage's letter is answered by the accompanying one from the unfortunate deluded lady to whom he cruelly and
shamelessly appeals, which she wrote to me on my acquainting her
with that part of his letter.   This is a subject of a delicate nature
on which I do not appeal to your Honourable Board, though one
professed object of your Government is the eradication of licentiousness and immorality.   It is, however, necessary for me to lay it
before you, as Mr Sage denies the assertion in my letter.   Be not
surprised that he should deny so obvious a truth when I acquaint
your Lordship and Gentlemen, that had I consented on a still more
delicate point, a solemn oath proffered on the sacrament would have
added perjury to the crimes of hypocrisy, falsehood, and violated
friendship.   I propose going to Europe as soon as I can settle my
private concerns, which business together with the employment to

which your Lordship and Gentlemen have been pleased to appoint me as Alderman in the Mayor's Court[1] will engross the whole of my time.   I therefore hereby request permission to resign the service of the Honourable Company.   Permit me at the same time to assure you, Honourable Masters, that I shall ever most heartily rejoice at the continued prosperity of the Company and retain a due sense of gratitude for the independent fortune which their service has enabled me to acquire; a fortune which I glory has been gained by industry and a lawful trade alone."

Letter of Anne Bolts to Mr William Bolts, dated the 6th November 1766:

"I have received your note informing me that Mr Sage in his letter to the Board denies having taken me from your house at Benares, and run away from the factory with me, alleging he was called down to the Court Martial, and appealing to me for the justification of his innocence.   I am sorry he has appealed to me, because as I imagine you will not let his letter to the Board go unanswered, I fear it will oblige you to produce this letter of mine. Yet as it is the only satisfaction I can give you and what justice requires I shall not hesitate to inform you that some time before the night he brought me away he had been employing the most wicked schemes to induce me to leave your house, sending me copies of what I was to write to him as if it came from myself, for his scheme was at first to have got me to run away by myself that he might execute his plan and not be brought to trouble.

Mr John Chamier who was in the scheme and through whose means our correspondence was carried on after the quarrel between you and Mr Sage had some days before my elopement advised me to pluck up courage on the occasion.

The evening Mr Sage came away with me he sent me two letters. In these letters he most vehemently exhorts me to come away, and after he came home from riding out, and you was gone abroad, I beckoned to him as he passed our house that I could not think of the scheme but called to him to come and speak to me.   Accordingly he came under my window and when he heard my disapprobation he flew into a most violent passion and began beating his head against a post that was opposite to my window intimidating me even with threats to comply with his imprudent plan.   Thus pressed and frightened I walked to the bottom of the garden and went out at the door where he met me and immediately put me into his 'fly palenqueen,'[2] which he had prepared and made his

[1] See page 42.
[2] Apparently a vehicle half-way between a palki and a fly, much like the modern "office ghari" of Calcutta, but without wheels.

servants take me away, he running by the side of the 'palenqueen' with me. He made his servants carry me to the water side, where he put me into a budgerow which he had furnished with necessaries, which budgerow Mr Sage had some days before borrowed from Mr Joseph Hare, and he brought me away in it to Patna. On the way down he told me he was afraid he should be turned out of the service for deserting the Company's affairs, but that he would say he was called down to Patna as an evidence to the Court Martial.

It is very true upon Sir Robert Fletcher's [1] arrival at Patna he did desire Mr Sage to appear as an evidence at his trial, but upon Mr Sage's representing that his evidence would be immaterial and desiring he might be off from attending, Sir Robert consented, and Mr Sage had had no intention of going as he informed me some time before, and besides to my certain knowledge he left Patna before the Court Martial came on.

I have been thus explicit in my letter not to exculpate my own imprudence in the part I acted, which will not admit of an excuse, but to detect Mr Sage's falsehood and hypocrisy after being the author of my ruin and the first publisher of my disgrace. I am with sincere wishes for your forgiveness of me.—Your affectionate wife.—ANNE BOLTS."

The character of Mrs Bolts is unconsciously exhibited in this curious narrative, and it is evident enough that her attempt to portray herself as the innocent victim of a designing villain will not bear examination. Nor do the conduct and utterance of Mr Bolts show the grief and indignation of the deeply injured husband whose domestic peace has been irreparably destroyed, though an allowance must, of course, be made for his origin and for a character strong, self-centred, and loveless. But it is not easy to understand the attitude of the Council towards his rival in his wife's affections, unless they had reason to suppose that Mr Bolts was guilty of the infamy of connivance in her desertion, and that the letter of November 6, 1766, was, in fact, dictated by her husband. Of this there is, however, no evidence, and the wording of the letter is on the whole inconsistent with such an hypothesis.

[1] See note on page 37.

Mrs Bolts, after this single document, disappears again from the records for some years. Whether she returned to her husband before he left Bengal, must be a matter of conjecture, therefore. In his petition, he does, indeed, refer to his "family" as present, when he was seized and carried off from his house in Calcutta; but this may refer to children only. At all events they were eventually reconciled, for after his return to India in 1779 Mrs Bolts appears as accompanying him and sharing with him the hospitality of the French consul at Surat. She died at Chandernagore on the 12th of September 1821, "en sa maison sur la ghatte," as the death certificate records. Her age at death is therein recorded as sixty-nine; but she was probably well over seventy, as she can hardly have been as young as twelve when she married. There were in Bengal in 1908 some twenty-five living descendants of Johan Carel Bolts, who died in 1809, and who may have been the son of William and Anne Bolts.

CHAPTER VIII

MR BOLTS'S APPOINTMENT AS ALDERMAN AND HIS RESIGNATION OF THE SERVICE

AN unaccountable feature of the Council's treatment of Mr Bolts, considering their frequently expressed disapproval of his conduct, the censure passed upon him by the Court of Directors, and the fact that he was actually under sentence of suspension at the time, is his elevation by the President and Council to the office of Alderman, or Judge, of the Mayor's Court in Calcutta, an office which conferred upon him a statutory right for life, and from which he could not be legally removed unless he should have been guilty of some offence constituting a just cause of dismissal. The appointment was made on the 11th of August 1766.

The Council and the Company had good cause later on to rue this extraordinary indiscretion.

In the same year the Select Committee formed a plan which would prevent junior civilians like Mr Bolts from making larger fortunes by private trade than some of the members of the Government were able to amass, an offence which in those days must have loomed large in the eyes of the gentlemen of the Council. Their ostensible object was, indeed, to protect the natives from oppression; but Mr Bolts was, perhaps, not very wrong in supposing that the unavowed motive was the more powerful in swaying the action of the majority, at least, of the Council.

The plan consisted of the formation of a great

official Inland Trade Society, which was to monopolise the lucrative private commerce hitherto enjoyed by individual civilians or associations of civilians.   All the salt, betel-nut, and tobacco, produced in or imported into Bengal, was to be sold exclusively to the Society, the inland trade in these articles being subjected to a duty payable to the Company at the rate of 35 per cent. for salt, 10 per cent. for betel-nut, and 25 per cent. for tobacco.

The shares in this Society were to be apportioned strictly according to the rank and station of each member in the Company's service.   All servants of the Company, except Writers, were to participate. A Committee of Trade was appointed to carry the plan into execution.   Accordingly we find an order passed by the Select Committee at their meeting of the 14th of October 1766,

"that the Secretary shall write to the Secretary of the Committee of Trade, directing him with the authority of his constituents to enrol Messrs Rumbold and Bolts in the list of proprietors of stock in the Inland Trade agreeably to their present station." [1]

One can easily imagine the feelings with which Mr Bolts, whose share as mere Factor would be one of the slenderest of all, received this announcement; and one of the motives of his subsequent resignation of the Company's service was, no doubt, the desire for "a position of greater freedom and less responsibility" for the prosecution of his extensive trading operations.

His partner, Mr Johnstone, complained bitterly to the President and Council, in a letter dated the 26th of August 1765, of the new monopoly and of the unfairness of being compelled to sell the firm's existing stock of salt to the Society of Trade at a price practically dictated by the latter.

[1] This scheme did not meet with the approval of the Directors, who forbade all private trade outside the Company's territories.

An incidental consequence arising out of Mr Sage's elopement with Mrs Bolts was a prolonged wrangle between Mr Bolts and the Council over the payment of his expenses in despatching from Benares to Patna the treasure deserted by Mr Sage.

On the 11th of December 1766 Mr Isaac Sage sends to the Council

"a bill upon Mr William Bolts for Rs. 8167/4/9 for grain sold by him out of the garrison of Chunar, and requests them to demand payment. Mr Bolts has refused to discharge the debt unless he is allowed to make a deduction of Rs. 100 for transporting some chests of treasure to Patna, the property of the Company; Mr Sage refused to allow this, as Mr Bolts had no kind of business to concern himself therewith."

"Ordered that . . . the Secretary be directed to demand the amount of the bill upon Mr Bolts together with interest from the day it was first tendered by Mr Sage."

In reply Mr Bolts sent in an account against the Company and a bill upon his Shroff[1] for the balance due to them.

On the 27th April 1767 the Council ordered

"that the Secretary do again demand the amount of the bill for the Company's grain . . . and that he do return the account current and bill upon the Shroff, acquainting Mr Bolts that the Company keep no open account with any individual, and if he has any demands on them, they are to be made separately; that he is therefore to apply to the buxy[2] for payment of the charges he was at in sending the treasure down from Benares. . . ."

Mr Bolts having repeated his former refusal to pay the Company's demand without deduction, the Council ordered the bill to be sent to the Honourable Company's lawyer, with orders to sue Mr Bolts in the Mayor's Court for the amount.

Two years later, in their letter of the 17th of March 1769, the Directors expressed their opinion of the litigation which ensued. The pertinacious Mr Bolts had meanwhile lost his case before the Mayor's

---

[1] Banker.   [2] Paymaster, treasurer.

Court and his appeal in Calcutta, but had again appealed to the Privy Council.

"We have considered the subject of your litigation with Mr Bolts respecting the Company's demand on him for grain delivered at Benares, and direct that you receive of his attorneys in Bengal the balance of his account with us, being Rs. 3175/7, which it appears from the proceedings he once tendered and was refused, and his solicitor here informs us he is still ready to pay on your demand.

Your proceedings in this affair have been laid before the Company's counsel, he is of opinion that when a cause is heard upon bill and answer without any replication, the answer must be admitted to be true, because without a replication no evidence can be brought by the defendant to prove the truth of any of the facts contained in such answer. That this is a fixed rule and that it cannot be otherwise is so obvious to common sense that he is convinced neither the Mayor's Court or the Governor in Council have the least doubt of it. They well know a party can't be deprived of his witnesses by the means of his antagonist in the suit, and then lose his cause for want of their testimony. If Mr Bolts has made a larger demand upon the Company, or given them credit for less than he ought in this cause, there is no remedy, the Company's agents are only to blame by their manner of conducting it. And he is clearly of opinion that under every circumstance of this case the judgment in favour of the Company is not to be supported. It is neither advisable nor prudent for the Company to bring this appeal before the Lords of the Council. If they should, he is convinced that the appellant will prevail and be decreed the whole of his demand."

Mr Bolts's resignation was accepted at the Council meeting of the 24th of November 1766. But though in his letter of resignation he had intimated his intention of returning to Europe as soon as he could settle his private concerns, "the trade of a country yet unexhausted was too lucrative to be easily relinquished," and he continued to embark upon fresh commercial ventures in addition to the extensive concerns in which he was already engaged. His continued residence and commercial activity in the dominions of Shuja-u-Daula were regarded with extreme disfavour by the Council, who had, no doubt reckoned on getting rid finally of a troublesome and dangerous intriguer, and were correspondingly disappointed and annoyed. Accordingly in January 1767 the Secretary was ordered to intimate to Mr Bolts that as he could not claim any title to remain longer in India, he was positively required not to engage further in commercial concerns, and to prepare to embark for England in one of the Company's returning ships of that season.

In reply to this communication Mr Bolts is able to make out a very plausible case for delay, and positively pledges himself to engage in no fresh commercial concerns and not to interfere in any way with the Company's investment.

He has several very considerable outstanding balances within the management of the Honourable Company, for the recovery of which he asks for perwannahs upon the different Zemindars, etc., concerned, directing them to summon his debtors to the district courts, and, after proof of the justice of his demands, to enforce payment. Here follow particulars of the debts in Purnea, Goraghat, Rangpur, Dinajpur, Jessore, etc., amounting to about Rs. 48,000. He has by sea and land, of his own and other people's, "about eight lacks of rupees now out, and actually employed in lawful trade, which noway interferes with the Honourable Company's investment." He has not lately, and will not enter into any new inland concerns, and he will engage, under any penalty, that no part of his trade shall, within the three Subahs,[1] in any shape, interfere with any part of the Honourable Company's investment. . . . He will never be guilty of any infringement of the laws of Great Britain, or the bye-laws of the Honourable Company where their jurisdiction extends; and out of their jurisdiction, he will freely submit to the customs and laws of

[1] Provinces, *i.e.* Bengal, Bihar, and Orissa.

the country. He requires only an equitable allowance of time, "to be indulged with those privileges which have ever been allowed, not only to gentlemen who have resigned, but those who have been dismissed the service." The Select Committee, at their meeting of the 3rd of March, conceded Mr Bolts's request, but strictly enjoined him to enter upon no fresh concerns, as the Board would expect implicit obedience to the orders he had already received. Letters were accordingly written to Shuja-u-Daula and Raja Bulwant Singh, who promised their assistance.

A week later these orders were modified to the extent that the President would only grant perwannahs on the courts of those districts where the demands were made, and that all demands made within the Company's jurisdiction should be examined and adjusted by the Collector-General.

CHAPTER IX

THE INTRIGUE AGAINST NOBKISSEN

MEANWHILE Mr Bolts had become engaged in an infamous conspiracy against Nobkissen in conjunction with .one Ramnant and the notorious Maharaja Nandkumar. Nobkissen had rendered great services to the English on board ship at Fulta after the capture of Calcutta, by supplying them with provisions at the risk of his life, the Nawab having prohibited it under penalty of death. These services induced Warren Hastings to take Nobkissen as his Munshi[1] and led to the subsequent elevation of his family. Mr Bolts sneeringly alludes to him as

"a man who from being the menial servant of Ramcharn, Governor Vansittart's banyan,[2] had raised himself to the dignity of Lord Clive's Persian writer, and with whom the Petitioner had never any connexions whatever."

Ramnant hatched a plot against the life of Nobkissen by falsely accusing him of having violated a Brahmin's wife. In his representation to the President, Nobkissen says:

"You, Sir, referred the affair to Mr Floyer,[3] the then Zemindar, and directed me to go to him for a clearing up of this matter. I obeyed and found Mr Bolts with Gokul and Kissen, the two brothers-in-law of Ram there.

Mr Floyer entered upon the business, when Gokul gave him a paper written in English containing an account of the complaint made against me, which Mr Bolts declared was a true translation he

---

[1] Persian translator and clerk. [2] Hindu clerk.
[3] One of the Members of Council.

had made from the Bengall.   Mr Floyer having read it aloud, Gokul swore to and signed it.[1]   Mr Floyer then asked Gokul if he had any witnesses, telling him 'now' is the proper time for their evidence.   Gokul replied, his brother Kissen; accordingly Kissen was called and sworn.

Mr Floyer was desirous of interrogating Kissen, but Mr Bolts interrupted him by saying that Kissen was ready to swear what was contained in the written paper already subscribed to by Gokul. Upon my requesting Mr Bolts might not interrupt, he bid me hold my tongue, nor desisted till the Zemindar ordered both to be silent. Mr Floyer then took Kissen's evidence and wrote the particulars with his own hand."

(There was a material difference in the respective depositions of Gokul and Kissen, though they lived in the same house and "had concocted the whole affair together.")   Finally, he begs leave to observe that the woman injured should surely have made her complaint to the Justice, and not done it by his (Nobkissen's) "avowed enemy, Mr Bolts."

In the trial Nobkissen was fully acquitted.

The Select Committee in their Proceedings of the 18th of April 1767 recorded their opinion of Mr Bolts's part in the plot against Nobkissen in the following terms :

"That Mr William Bolts appears from many circumstances to be deeply concerned in the conspiracy to ruin Nobkissen's character and attempt his life, in which opinion the Committee are confirmed by his violent and declared resentment to Nobkissen, by the share he took in stirring up and instigating the prosecution against him in the Zemindary court upon an imaginary and false accusation, and particularly from his taking at this juncture into his service Ramnant, a man who stands publicly convicted of perjury, *with a view of forging and publishing further aspersions upon Nobkissen's character*.[2]   That Mr Bolts having upon this and many other occasions endeavoured to draw an odium upon the Administration and to promote faction and discontent in the settlement, has rendered himself unworthy of any

---

[1] Gokul's deposition is reproduced in full in Mr Bolts's tract, in which he gives his version of the affair of Ramnant and Nobkissen: see page 119.

[2] Vide Mr Bolts's comment on this remarkable indictment by hypothesis, page 94.

D

further indulgence from the Committee and of the Company's protection. That therefore he be directed to quit Bengal and to proceed to Madras by the first ship that shall sail for that presidency in the month of July next, in order to take his passage from thence to Europe in September."

On the same occasion they censured and punished Nandkumar in the following resolution :

"That Nundcoomar appearing to have instigated and forged accusations against Nobkissen by large promises of money and presents, with a view of gratifying his personal resentment and indulging an intriguing disposition, shall be ordered by the President strictly to confine himself to his own house, and in future to avoid such practices on pain of forfeiting the Company's protection and being delivered over to the Government for such punishment as his crimes may be thought to deserve."

This was seven years before Nandkumar was employed as the instrument of Philip Francis's rancorous hatred against Warren Hastings.

CHAPTER X

MR BOLTS'S CONTUMACY

ON the 24th of August 1767, the Board resumed operations against Mr Bolts, who had entirely disregarded their previous orders:

"Mr Bolts not having complied with our orders for his return to Europe on some ship of the last season, ordered that the Secretary do inform him that the *Lord Holland* will be despatched for England in the course of next month, and that we positively insist on his proceeding by that ship."

A sarcastic reply from Mr Bolts to the Secretary followed. Alluding to the Board's resolution of the 24th, he is

"surprised that the gentlemen should think it necessary to repeat their orders so frequently in a matter which he is much more desirous of performing than they can be supposed to be of seeing performed, while there are so many others in a similar situation who are never thought of."

On the same date, the 29th of August, he informed the Board that he had received their orders to return on the *Lord Holland*, but that he found himself unable to comply with them, as his affairs were not yet in order, though he longed "to breathe the air of liberty in his *native* country," unless the Board would indemnify him and all those whose business agent he was for any losses sustained by his departure. He also alludes to his address of the 7th of February to the Select Committee, showing that he has realised only 1½ lakhs out of 8 lakhs of his own and other people's property entrusted to him; he now adds that another 8 lakhs of trust property is still unrealised. He proposes (1) that the property of William Hay, deceased, should be remitted to England by Council bills—as a favour to the family of the murdered man,[1] and (2) that the commercial concerns should be purchased at a reasonable price by the members of the Board who belong to the Inland Trade Societies.

These two letters were not considered by the Board until the 1st of October; their resolution on them refused further indulgence, and repeated the order to embark on the next ship that sailed for Europe. Meanwhile he was positively forbidden to leave Calcutta without their express permission.

"Ordered also that the Mayor's Court be acquainted herewith. that they may apply for another alderman in his room."

On the 9th of October Mr Bolts responded with a decorous defiance of the Board's orders.

As the Secretary has not answered the material part of his letter, he begs leave to refer to it and to request an answer.

He refuses to leave India this season, unless he receives a satisfactory answer regarding his commercial concerns and the property for which he is trustee.

As to the accusation that he is carrying on an improper intercourse with the Dutch,[2] he asserts that it is utterly false and baseless. He demands to be confronted with his accusers, and piques himself, notwithstanding the injustice with which he has been treated, upon having as sincere a regard for the interest of the Company as any member of the Board. Referring to the "contradictory and insulting order" of the Select Committee, not to leave Calcutta without express permission, he hopes the Board will cancel

[1] He was one of the victims of the Patna massacre, 1763.
[2] See pages 65 to 67.

it. Meanwhile the Board had met with a severe rebuff from the Mayor's Court. They had written to the Court to inform them that they had

"directed Mr William Bolts, now an alderman of their Court, to proceed to Europe by the next ship that sails from hence. They give the Honourable Court this notice that they may if they please apply for an alderman in his room, and to acquaint them on their so doing their request shall be immediately complied with."

Mr Bolts thereupon addressed a letter to the Mayor and Aldermen of the Mayor's Court, in which he vigorously inveighed against the tyranny of the President and Council. He has heard, he says, of the extraordinary attempt of the Governor and Council to remove him from his seat as alderman, in defiance of the King's charter; he is glad to learn the just disregard with which this attempted infringement of British liberties has been treated; had the attempt succeeded, British subjects would have been as easily deprived of their property and fortunes as in the present despotic reign they have been of their liberties and every British privilege.

The act is really the personal act of the President, Verelst, though nominally that of President and Council.

"How deplorable would have been our situation, if at the base desire of a Governor, or even a Governor and his Council, the express orders of the charter should be set aside and a free British subject exposed to be deprived of his honour and liberty."

He defies the President and Council legally to disqualify him from holding his honourable seat at their Court, and he is confident that the Court will never suffer him to be otherwise dismissed.

He concludes with a request for a copy of the "extraordinary" letter of the President and Council.

On the same date, the 8th of October, Mr Bolts addressed a letter to two members of Council, Messrs Richard Becher and James Alexander; he appeals to

them "as new and unprejudiced members, not to
allow their minds to be poisoned against him by the
other 'interested' members of the Board, especially as
they have heard nothing on the other side." His
object is to set them on their guard against the
artifices of many combined against one, through
private interest, private and personal connections, and
intrigues.

He hopes he may not be forced in his own defence
"to print and publish to the world at home what may
add to the national odium against the Company."

This is the first hint of those volumes, "Considerations on India Affairs," in which Mr Bolts so successfully fulfilled his object of "adding to the national
odium against the Company."

Meanwhile, as a preliminary to an appeal to the
Press, Mr Bolts addressed to the Court of Directors
an appeal against the Council's recent orders.

The Register of the Mayor's Court replied to the
Secretary that when Mr Bolts's seat as an alderman
became vacant, the Court would apply to the Honourable the President and Council to appoint another
gentleman to fill up the vacancy.

To complete the discomfiture of the Council, the
Company's attorney informed them four days later of
the rejection by the Mayor's Court of his motion "that
Mr Bolts might give especial bail" after the judgment
on the grain case had been given in favour of the
Company.

On the 18th of October Mr Bolts wrote to the
Council requesting the transmission of an accompanying address to the Court of Directors in vindication of
his character and conduct. The following extracts
will give a sufficient indication of the nature of this
document :

"It is doubtless a hardy attempt for me . . . to make a public
attack on the President when the majority of his secret Committee

and Council are also parties concerned, but a regard to my character obliges me to it, and as I have on my side truth and facts which are obstinate and hard to bend, I dare in this impolitic and uncustomary manner brave the envenomed shafts of future oppression and injustice, which cannot exceed in malignancy those I have already unconcerned sustained."

He adds that the majority of the Council are new-comers, ignorant of the natives and of the vernaculars, and therefore, no doubt, misled by his enemies.

He offers to explain or prove to the Board any points in his memorial to the Directors.

CHAPTER XI

MR BOLTS'S INTRIGUE WITH THE NAWAB OF OUDH

SOME months before his quarrel with the President and Council came to a head, Mr Bolts had begun making friends of the mammon of unrighteousness by means of a correspondence with M. Gentil, a French adventurer, high in favour with the Nawab, and even with the Nawab himself. One of his letters to M. Gentil fell into the hands of Mr Maddison, the Company's Agent at Patna, who transmitted it to Governor Verelst through Colonel Smith, one of the members of the .Select Committee. The translation of the letter submitted to the Select Committee ran as follows :

"*June* 19, 1767.

"DEAR SIR,—It is a long time since I heard from you, which has made me a little uneasy. I have long intended to come from hence to have the pleasure of seeing you, as also to pay my respects to the Nabob. But my affairs have not yet permitted me. Nevertheless it's what I hope to be able to do in a short time.

In regard to the saltpetre, I hope the disputes on that subject are ended. But it is not possible for me to abandon my right for the advantage of other gentlemen who have no other pretensions than what are founded on injustice, and who would take the advantage of my absence to deprive me of the advantages of my contracts, which have existed a long time, and which were drawn out with all propriety and justice conformable to the customs of merchants.

If that had been for the Nabob, it would have been another thing ; but before I give up the point to gentlemen who are not anyways my superiors, I assure you I will follow the affair to the last Court of Justice, where I can have recourse. Next year I'll give over all further commerce, but in the meantime I hope you will help me with your assistance.

My gomastah, Gocul Dass, writes me that you had informed him that Colonel Barker had wrote letters to stop all my business and drive my people away. I shall be obliged to you for your information on that subject, for that gentleman is not authorised to act in such a manner.

I have taken the liberty to send your letter for Coja Rafael.[1] I beg you will deliver it to him and send me his answer. I am surprised the Nabob has not yet paid the amount of the broadcloth which my people sold him. If that is true, be so good as to represent the same to him. Melcomb[1] writes me that he also hath sent some cloth from Dacca to the Nabob's camp. I don't doubt of your favourable assistance for the sale."

He next offers to reciprocate the good turn, and assures him of his good-will, and concludes :

"I have wrote a letter to the Nabob, to whom I beg you will give my humble respects.

There is arrived an English Europe ship and another French one. The affairs of the Company are in great agitation and are laid before the King and Parliament of England, and according to the letters I have received, there is great likelihood that my associate, Mr Johnstone, will come out Governor from the King.

I shall be glad, from time to time, to hear from you, whom am with a most perfect esteem.—Dear Sir, Your most obedient servant.—WILLIAM BOLTS."

The last paragraph of this curious composition is worth quoting in the original :

"J'ai écrit une lettre au Navab a qui je vous prie de faire me tres humble respects ; nous avons eu un vaisseau d'Europe Anglois, et un autre François : les affaires de notre Compagne sont dans une grande agitation devant le Roi et le parlement d'Angleterre ; et selon les lettres que j'ai reçu il a grande apparance qui mon Associe Monsieur Johnstone viendra Gouverneur de la part du Roi. Je serai charmé de reçevoir de temps en temps de vos nouvelles qui suis avec une parfait considération,—Mon cher Monsieur, Votre tres humble Serviteur.—GUILLAUME BOLTS."

On the 23rd of October 1767 Colonel Smith reported as follows to the Select Committee :

"I remember to have mentioned in Committee that Mons. Gentil

---

[1] Armenian agents of Mr Bolts.

waš a very improper person to be with Sujah al Dowlah. I am fully convinced of this, and wish some mode could be thought on to have him removed. The person who has had the establishment of Sujah al Dowlah's artillery is one of Mons. Gentil's comrades, and formerly was an officer in the French service."

On the 11th of December, in transmitting Mr Bolts's intercepted letter, he writes :

"The nature of the intelligence transmitted from Calcutta by Sujah al Dowlah's Vakeel [1] is without limits ; the Nabob is almost as fully acquainted with the Parliamentary proceedings concerning the Company's affairs as I am. How far the importance and dignity of the Company and the weight and influence of administration are lessened in his esteem by this communication, may be easily conceived. Whilst a Vakeel is so easy and so sure a Channel to communicate intelligence, few men will be found so hardy as to maintain a direct correspondence with the Nabob; but there is a man who has obliquely offered so great an insult to our President, that, was I present at the Board, I would move for the exertion of our authority to the utmost extent, to free the settlement from so dangerous an inhabitant. I mean Mr Bolts: [2] and the enclosed copy of a letter to Monsieur Gentil (the original is in my possession) residing in Sujah al Dowlah's court, wherein he asserts an absolute falsehood, which tends to lessen that essential dignity and necessary influence of our President, is surely deserving of your severest resentment. Nor is this the only letter he wrote; for the Nabob acquainted a person of undoubted honour, that Mr Bolts had wrote the same to Meer Mushallah, formally physician and

---

[1] Solicitor.
[2] In a subsequent minute dated the 4th of May 1768 Colonel Smith wrote : "It appears . . . that Mr Bolts ever since your resolution of the 5th November has been corresponding with the Country powers ; this correspondence is wisely and expressly prohibited to individuals by the orders of our Honble. Masters. If you had not already entered into a resolution of sending Mr Bolts to Europe, most undoubtedly I would have made such a motion. But when I read an unanimous decree of your Board for taking such measures on this occasion as appears absolutely necessary for the publick service, I cannot but conjure you, Gentlemen, to support the dignity of Government by enforcing obedience to your own Resolutions. For should we suffer Mr Bolts with impunity to bid defiance to your authority, the consequences are so very obvious that to mention them is unnecessary. I do therefore move that the Resolution of the 5th November 1767 shall be carried into execution, and in case of disobedience to your orders on the part of Mr Bolts, that he shall positively be sent prisoner to Europe on the first ship which shall be despatched from this presidency."

confidant of Cossim Ally, from whom the Nabob heard it. Here-after I may lay before you other proofs of the extent of the intelligence communicated through the Vakeel."

On the 5th of November the President laid the following minute before the Board :

"Mr Bolts's address to the Court of Directors is a convincing proof of the propriety of the Committee's resolutions regarding him ; it is full of palpable misrepresentations and falsehoods, and the personal invectives levelled at the President will obtain no credence from those aequainted with his character and conduct."

He then refers to a previous minute of his own for his reason for bringing the complaint against Nobkissen before the Select Committee.

With regard to the surrender of Ramnant to the Government on the recommendation of the Select Committee, in order that he might be made accountable for his "extortions and villainies," he observes that Mr Bolts's assertion, that the only demands made on Ramnant during his imprisonment were for debts due to the President, is false :

"I positively forbid any demands being made upon my account until full and ample restitution had been obtained for the sufferers from Ramnant's extortions at Malda. I have not received a single rupee . . . of the debt. Ministers, Mr Sykes, and many others can testify to the truth of this denial."

He has never had any business concerns at Dinajpur.

He repudiates Mr Bolts's imputation of an improper motive for his action in the case of Gokul Suna.

He leaves it to the Council to punish this insult to the President : he will not vote himself.

Thereupon the Board resolved :

"That we unanimously support the President's conduct of this case, resent the insult offered to him and the Government in Mr Bolts's insolent and libellous attack on the President and in his factious attempt to sow discord in the Council."

They are all determined to punish Mr Bolts's attempt

"to sap the foundations of all government, to subvert by the factious cry of liberty the principles of surbordination, and to loosen all those sacred ties whereby men are united together in society,"

and therefore resolve :

"That our former orders to Mr Bolts for proceeding to England shall be repeated, and that in case of disobedience to and contempt for our authority his person shall be seized and forcibly sent home a prisoner in one of the ships of this season."

The correspondence is to be sent home to the Directors to justify the Council's action and to convince the Directors that

"unless they will vindicate their own authority as exercised in unavoidable acts by their representatives in India and assert the privileges of their royal charter, their settlements and government must infallibly be precipitated into anarchy and confusion."

To this resolution Mr Floyer appended a minute defending himself against a false imputation made against him by Mr Bolts with regard to Nobkissen's trial. The Select Committee were evidently impressed by Colonel Smith's warning about M. Gentil's position at the court of Oudh, for they promptly wrote to inform the Colonel that they had recommended to the President that he should take effectual steps for removing M. Gentil and his associates from the Court and Councils of Shuja-u-Daula; "which we hope to effect," they add,

"without laying a disagreeable restraint on the Nabob's inclinations. The measure becomes necessary, but we are desirous of observing on this, as upon all other occasions, the most punctilious delicacy towards his highness."[1]

The following extract from the report sent by

[1] In spite of several applications to him, the Nawab could not be prevailed upon to remove M. Gentil from his court, though in September 1769 he went so far as to tell Captain Harper that if war with France ensued, he should feel bound to give him up.

Mr Maddison to the President is instructive as showing the nervous apprehensions of embroilment with the Company's servants which the Nawab entertained. After explaining how he got Mr Bolts's letter to M. Gentil into his hands, Mr Maddison says that he made an effort, unhappily unsuccessful, to get hold of Mr Bolts's letter to the Nawab :

"At last I took occasion one day, when the Nabob was enquiring what news from Europe, to tell him that we had no news which could be depended on; and that the intelligence Mr Bolts had communicated to him, concerning Mr Johnstone coming out Governor on the part of the King, was certainly erroneous. He answered me with precipitation, 'No, no, he did not write it to me, he wrote it to Meer Mushullah, and I had it from him."

Referring to the Armenian gomastahs of Mr Bolts as channels of intelligence to the Nawab, he describes them as

"perpetually filling the country and the Nabob's court with lying rumours; they have reported that Mr Bolts was returning to Benares with greater power than before, that he was even set out, and a variety of other falsehoods, in order to mislead the Nabob. . . . The Armenians, indeed, in general, seem to have adopted a system of fixing themselves in the Nabob's dominions, as they were formerly at Moorshedabad; and though the Nabob has, on account of some of their malpractices, forbid them his province, yet, as English gomastahs, he is, perhaps, cautious of expelling them. . . . I learnt a circumstance at Benares concerning Mr Bolts's manner of passing his fleets, which may not be improper to communicate. He procured last year a considerable number of dustucks from Mr Middleton, for saltpetre, tincal,[1] etc., and as some of these dustucks have lately been seen in Coja Melcombe's hands, it is probable he avails himself of these."

When the Board met on the 10th of December, the President presented the following minute on Mr Bolts's intrigues :

"The President acquaints the Board that he has from time to time received information of the improper correspondence carried on by Mr Bolts with Sujah al Dowlah, Mr Gentil, and many other persons, that he desired a gentleman residing up the country to

---

[1] Borax.

endeavour to procure a particular letter written by Mr Bolts, which
he effected and delivered the letter to Colonel Smith, who enclosed
the same to the Committee; that he can assert from undoubted
authority that Mr Bolts continues his correspondence with persons
residing at the Courts of the Country princes and with his Armenian
agents, endeavouring by false reports and representations to lessen
the respect due to the present Administration and to destroy the
harmony and confidence between us and the Powers of Indostan."

Through various Armenian agents, he is endeavouring to injure the interests of those in whose service
he made a fortune. When in the Company's service
he procured dastaks on the pretext of wanting them
to pass his goods, but kept them by him unused until
his resignation. Ever since he has used them to
carry on his trade duty free. The President has
therefore written to the ministers asking them to stop
all dastaks of ancient date.

Colonel Smith followed with a contemptuous
reference to Mr Bolts's charge against himself:

"Colonel Smith was and continues of opinion that whatever is
said by Mr Bolts is too much below his contempt to deserve an
answer. But the Colonel imagines that words cannot point out
the calumniating disposition of this man in a stronger point of
view than the declaration contained in his own letter . . . wherein
he insinuates to the Company as if the Emperor Shah Alum was
kept as a prisoner in the English camp. To endeavour to refute
such an assertion would be to give it an air of credibility. The
whole army and every man in the Colony who knows anything of
the circumstance, knows it to be utterly false and without the
smallest foundation, and it could only be such a man as Mr Bolts
who would publicly set his name to what he himself must know to
be an infamous falsehood. And the Colonel is only surprised
that whilst this man is arraigning the characters of every member of
this administration, he has invented nothing worse against him."

REPORT TO THE DIRECTORS

At the same meeting of the Board a report on Mr
Bolts's proceedings was included in their despatch to
the Directors:

"We are now come to a subject which calls for your most serious

consideration : it relates to the conduct of Mr William Bolts, lately
in your service, and we think it proper to introduce it here, as it
requires a full execution of the privileges granted in the royal charter
to you, and delegated to your representatives in India, to represent
in a proper manner the insult given to our government in the person
of our President, and the daring attempt not only to lessen our
influence in the country, whereby your influence would infallibly
suffer, but also to destroy that harmony which now so happily
prevails in your councils. These purposes, so unnatural to a British
subject, who had acquired an opulent fortune in your service, Mr
Bolts has attempted to effect by personal addresses to our Board,
and secret correspondences carried on through the means of
Armenian agents at the courts of Sujah al Dowlah and of other
princes.

We acquainted you, in our last letter, that, in consequence of a
resolution taken by the Select Committee regarding Mr Bolts, we
had sent him positive orders to return to Europe this season. Some
time after, we received a long letter from Chinsura,[1] at which place
he frequently resided for some time past, informing us, with much
freedom of style, that, if we would take his concerns and those
of his constituents off his hands, he would comply with our
directions.

The insolence of his reply induced us not only to repeat our
orders, but, on his return to town, to forbid him quitting the colony
until the time of his embarkation arrived ; in defiance of which he
immediately withdrew from the Presidency, and returned to Chinsura,
from whence he sent us a most insulting letter, reflecting on the
character of the President and of several of the members of our
Board. This was accompanied by a long address to you, the
absurdity and malice of which is too evident to require any strictures
from us : we shall therefore forward it without remark a number in
the packet. The measures we had recourse to on this occasion
were these ; first, unanimously to assure the President, that we
approved the whole of his conduct during the course of his proceedings with regard to Mr Bolts, and that we entertained the warmest
resentment against Mr Bolts for presuming upon so libellous and
unjust an attack upon our Governor ; and next to determine on
repeating our peremptory orders to him to proceed to Europe without delay ; with which if he refuses compliance, we shall seize him
by force, and send him prisoner by one of the ships of this season.
The expediency of fulfilling this resolution becomes more evident
from the intelligence which we have since received of his informing
Monsieur Gentil, a Frenchman at the Court of Sujah al Dowlah, by
letter, that the Company's affairs in Europe were in the utmost con-

---

[1] According to Mr Bolts, he himself delivered this letter in Calcutta.

fusion; and that his *associate*[1] Mr Johnstone, as he terms him, would be appointed Governor here on the part of His Majesty. An attested copy of this letter appears on our consultations, and the original is now in the hands of Colonel Smith. Several other letters to different people in power at the Hindostan Courts have been seen."

---

[1] "Associé" should have been rendered "partner," as Mr Bolts clearly meant. The misrepresentation appears somewhat disingenuous.

CHAPTER XII

MR BOLTS'S ALLEGED INTRIGUE WITH THE DUTCH

OWING to his Dutch birth, Mr Bolts was peculiarly liable to suspicion in his relations with the agents of the Dutch Company, a suspicion which was naturally strengthened by his flight to the Dutch factory at Chinsura when he was threatened with arrest in Calcutta.

In September 1767 Mr Kelsall, Chief of Dacca, addressed a report concerning Mr Bolts's doings at Dacca to the President of the Select Committee, the tenor of which went to show that Mr Bolts's intercourse with the agents of the Dutch Company boded as ill to the interests of the East India Company as his previous intrigue with the Court of Shuja-u-Daula, which has been narrated above:

"In a letter I had the honour to address to you in the month of May last, I mentioned, though in a cursory manner, the footing on which the Dutch had then newly established their factory at Dacca, not, as the event has shown, to transact business on behalf of their Company, but, under the sanction of public authority, to fulfil a private compact of Messrs Vernet[1] and Bolts."

The late Dutch Resident, he continues, Mr Lankheet, disdained to accept a commission on such terms, whereupon he was superseded. His successor, when he found, instead of a representative of the Company, that he was sent up in the capacity of a mere gomastah, to fulfil a private engagement, in like

---

[1] President of the Dutch factory at Chinsura.

manner declined it.   Both these gentlemen have ever
since been violently persecuted by Mr Vernet.

"Here is an Armenian, one Coja Miguel Sarties, a man that has
before done business for Mr Bolts, who, not so scrupulous as the
Dutch gentlemen, has made no difficulty of accepting the commission. The business is now in his hands, and, to fulfil it, he has had
made over to him a sum to the amount of near seven lacks of
rupees ; so enormous a sum I should have thought even beyond the
conscience even of an Armenian to presume to invest, and should
have doubted my information, if I had not received it from the best
authority, one of the Dutch gentlemen.

I have thought it my duty to give you this intelligence, and trust,
Sir, you will take measures for defeating the intentions of Messrs
Vernet and Bolts, and of the Armenian their agent, which must
materially prejudice our Company's business and the trade in
general, since in order to get in their investment, they must
necessarily purchase at an advanced price."

The President did not communicate this information
to the Board till nearly a year later, apparently because
he was endeavouring to obtain written confirmation
from Mr Lankheet of Mr Kelsall's report.   In a postscript, dated the 19th September, to the Council's letter
to the Directors of the 12th of September 1768 they
remark :

" The President this day laid before us a letter he received from the
Chief at Dacca concerning Mr Bolts assisting the Dutch in procuring
their investment, and acquainted us he has for some time past had
intimation of the subject on which it treats.   But not having been
able to procure authentic proofs regarding it, he deferred recording
it until this time.   He is still endeavouring to gain every other information in his power, which you shall be fully acquainted with
in our future advices."

The subsequent correspondence on this subject
shows that the Board were unsuccessful in their attempt
to procure the necessary affidavit, and the charge
therefore, though circumstantially probable, remained
unproven.   Writing in March 1770, the Directors
observe that they have received a declaration of Mr
Thomas Kelsall, on oath, reciting a conversation

that passed between him and Mr Daniel Lankheet relative to a clandestine trade carried on at Dacca between Mr Bolts and Mr Vernet, to a very great amount, in prejudice to the Company's investment,

"but as this representation is not authenticated either by Mr Lankheet's affidavit or any other evidence, we cannot make any use of it in justification for your sending Mr Bolts to England in the manner you did. But we hope and expect that you have made a very strict enquiry into this affair and punished such of our servants as have been found guilty of such notorious infidelity to their employers, and we desire you will not fail to transmit the whole of your proceedings in this respect to us, authenticated in the clearest and fullest manner, so as to be made use of as evidence in the Courts of Record here, if there should be any necessity so to do in order to obtain justice and satisfaction to the Company for this offence. Mr Lankheet's information at large upon oath touching this transaction seems to be the most material evidence, and we hope you will be able to obtain it."

In reply to this despatch the Board regret being unable to procure Mr Lankheet's affidavit; no Company's servant, they add, is implicated in the transaction, only Mr Bolts.

CHAPTER XIII

"WILLING TO WOUND"

IT was not till the summer of 1768 that the crisis of the struggle between Mr Bolts and the Government was reached. In spite of his disregard of their repeated orders to leave India, the Council hesitated for many months to follow up their threat of forcible expulsion. During this intervening period, however, the Government resorted to very strong measures, not always legally defensible, to prevent Mr Bolts from collecting his outstanding balances. His agents were seized and imprisoned ; their petitions and his remonstrances were alike disregarded. In a personal correspondence with Mr Bolts, Mr Verelst somewhat disingenuously replied to his protests with the assertion that he had given no special orders to impede his business :

March 3, 1768. MR VERELST TO MR BOLTS

"I have received your letter of the 30th instant, and am to acquaint you that *I know of no orders for impeding the business of your gomastahs in particular,* in the dominions of Sujah al Dowlah or Bulwant Sing. Repeated complaints have been received from those two princes of the oppressive conduct of gomastahs taking the English name and carrying on trade in their countries. The honourable Company have been pleased to express their orders for a positive prohibition to their servants of all trade whatever in those provinces,[1] and the Presidency of Fort William have resolved to put a stop to it in future, by a recall of all such gomastahs. How far, or by what right, your gomastahs can be allowed to continue there after the time already allotted you for the adjustment of your concerns, must be determined by the Government here."

---

[1] See page 43, note.

This statement is clearly inconsistent, as Mr Bolts subsequently pointed out in paragraph 17 of his petition to the Directors, with the minute issued by Mr Verelst in the previous December, in which, after censuring three of Mr Bolts's Armenian agents by name, he notes that the President and Council have desired the Nawab "to banish all such as are in his country under the pretexts of being gomastahs to the English."

Indeed Mr Verelst's actual communication to Nawab Shuja-u-Daula went much further than mere generalities. In his letter to the Nawab, of the 27th of February 1768, there is a separate enclosure in which he directly requests the Nawab to apprehend, or order Captain Harper to apprehend, and send down to Calcutta the two Armenians "Coja Rafael and Coja Estevan," and significantly adds : "As there is no separation between us, I doubt not you will oblige in this matter." Moreover, the select Committee had written previously to Colonel Smith, on the 22nd of December 1767, urging him to use his "utmost endeavours with the Nabob to remove Mr Bolts's gomastahs" from his dominions. The report of the Select Committee on the abuse of the gomastah system, issued in May 1768, while suggesting "an indulgence of two months' time to enable merchants to settle their affairs," recommended that orders should be issued "for effectually preventing in future any trade being carried on beyond the Provinces by gomastahs assuming the English name."

In a letter dated the 27th July Mr Bolts represented his grievance to the Board with remarkable freedom of style.

On behalf of his agents, Coja Gregore, Coja-maul, Coja Melcomb, and Cojee Johannes Padre Rafael, he takes the liberty of troubling them with this address, forced by duty to maintain their cause who solely on his account have suffered a long and severe imprisonment, and are likely to be totally ruined, and in hopes that the particular sufferings of these men may excite their compassion to action in rescuing them and their families from the total ruin which threatens them.

On the 15th May [1] past the relations of Cojee Gregore and Cogee Melcomb did themselves the honour of presenting an address to the Board which they delivered to the President, informing the Board of the distresses they laboured under by the imprisonment and detention of their persons then at Muxabad. On the 23rd May following they were released from their confinement and arrived in Calcutta on the 8th June—Cogee Melcomb having been confined in all from the 12th of March to the 23rd May, being two months and nine days. On the 10th of June they waited upon the President to thank him for their releasement, and among other things

"acquainted him of their having acted upon the authority of perwannahs under the seal of the Honourable the United English East India Company of which perwannahs are in my possession, and one of them being on a subsequent day shown to the President in consequence of his request he was pleased to put it in his pocket. Upon observing it was registered he became angry and thereupon absolutely refused to grant the necessary perwannahs for recovering their effects, though the said President had been pleased to give perwannahs also upon the Nabob Mahomed Reza Cawn, Rajah Shitabroy, and the Rajah Bulwan Sing in favour of a French gentleman named Mons. Canouge that came down under confinement from Patna to Muxàdavad in company with the said Armenians

---

[1] Soon after their seizure Mr Bolts had applied to the President for their release ; the latter referred him to the Select Committee, who refused to grant him any assistance. On the 18th of April he addressed the Board and was not vouchsafed any reply. A subsequent application of the Nawab of Bengal of the 2nd of May was similarly treated ; but the Board were moved to repeat their resolution of the previous November to send Mr Bolts home by the next ship. On the 10th of May Mr Bolts responded with a formal protest against the President and Council through the Notary Public, which the latter presented to the Board on the 18th of May.

and was in consequence of the said perwannahs immediately released and permitted to return up the country to collect his effects. Cogee Johannes Rafael has likewise in the same manner been seized, taken from his effects and from the management of the concerns with which he was entrusted, and confined ever since the 27th March past being according to my last advices still detained in confinement at Muxadavad. In the meantime a publication has been made by the authority of your Honourable Board prohibiting not only the English and their dependents, but also all Armenians and the descendants of the Armenians living under the Company's protection from trading directly or indirectly out of the provinces of Bengal, Bahar, and Orixa under the penalty of the utmost severe punishment and of the seizure and confiscation of their property."

These unhappy merchants have their whole fortunes dispersed in those prohibited districts; they are amenable for the very large outstanding concerns which they were entrusted with the management of; they never knew, or were acquainted with, the above orders and prohibitions till they were lately issued, long before which by their sudden seizure and imprisonment they were taken from their habitations and obliged to leave everything exposed to plunder and ruin; they dare not attempt to interfere for fear of corporal punishment and the confiscation of their property. In the meantime they are not conscious of any crime, but on the contrary are certain they have never in the most distant manner injured the Company nor given the Board any cause to be displeased with them. Numbers of other English agents and gomastahs are not only still permitted, but protected in residing within the provinces of Oud, Illahabad, and Banaras from whence these merchants have been forcibly brought.

Though the President and Members of the Board have assured him they knew nothing of any orders for the confinement of these merchants, yet the Country Governors pretend they have received such orders. He therefore asks for letters to be sent to "the Nabob Mahomed Reza Cawn, Rajah Shitabroy, Rajah

Bulwan Sing, and the Nabob Shuja al Dowlah " to
enable those merchants to finish their concerns, and to
collect and bring down their effects without fear of
corporal punishment or confiscation of their properties.

" As you have already acquainted me with your determinations [1]

---

[1] This refers to the resolution of the Board at their meeting of the
18th of April 1768 : " As Mr Bolts from a series of misconduct and
bad behaviour hath been deemed unworthy of and forfeited all title to
the Company's protection, and it has in consequence been withdrawn
from him, and as orders have been repeatedly issued from this Board for
him to quit the country and sufficient time has been allowed him to
adjust his affairs, we shall not interfere or interest ourselves in his affairs,
nor has he the least right to expect the assistance he claims of us.

Agreed, therefore, that no further notice be taken of these letters from
Mr Bolts than being recorded upon our consultations."

The last of Mr Bolts's letters herein referred to was addressed to
Governor Verelst by name, and dated the 18th of April 1768. It
employs the language of direct menace to the head of the Government :

" SIR,—In my last letter to you of the 11th instant, I acquainted you
that Shitabroy the Company's Collector at Patna had there confined
sundry of my agents, whereby I am likely to be a loser of one hundred
and fifty thousand rupees, and requested of you a letter ordering him to
release them, and not receiving any answer and to avoid troubling you
continually on the subject, on the 13th instant I wrote a letter to Mr
John Knott, your Secretary, who informed me that upon his communi-
cating it to you, you referred me for the answer to my application
to the Secretary of the Select Committee. I accordingly made application to Mr Charles Floyer, who yesterday sent me a letter of which
the enclosed is a copy informing me that the resolution of the Select
Committee was that no protection should be granted to me, and that
they were determined not to interfere in obtaining for me the redress
required.

As I am not to be trifled with, I must inform you that I am expecting
commissions from the High Court of Chancery, which will not only put
it out of any man's power to screen himself behind the garb assumed
under the names of ' Nabob and Country Government,' but also force
into light the most secret proceedings of the Junto called Select Committee in all things wherein the character, liberty, property, or life of a
British subject is concerned.

And reflect, Sir, that as I am very averse to disputes and litigations,
it is yet in your power, by giving me only the letter I have required, to
prevent things going to extremities, thereby preserving yourself and
others from many ruinous and shameful consequences, and your
employers from national dishonour. I therefore request that after due
consideration you will please to acquaint me in answer to this, whether
or not you will give me the letters I have required, or whether the
sentiments contained in Mr Floyer's beforesaid letter are such as you
avow, and esteem a final answer to the complaints I have made to you."

not to interfere with what concerns me in particular, please to
remark that I only make this my last application, as is incumbent
upon me, in behalf of my injured servants."

By the intelligence he has obtained from Benares,
and the information of Mons. Canouge, he is convinced that the President, whatever he may have
persuaded the rest of the Board of, did himself actually
give the orders for the confinement of the above said
agents, particularly to Raja Bulwant Singh. For Mr
Verelst on a presumption that the Raja had made
public and given copies of the several orders sent to
him, wrote to him a very severe perwannah forbidding
him ever to furnish any one with copies of the orders
he should send him. And for the same reason the
Raja's Ambassador has been lately disgraced, and the
Raja informed that he was dismissed and ordered
away from Calcutta.

" The consequences of the disgraceful dismission of an ambassador
are obvious. But if I could not prove it to be fact I should hardly
think it credible that the President's private pique and motives for
screening himself in my affair should have carried him such lengths,
as to risk the friendship of so powerful a frontier ally as the Rajah
Bulwan Sing, at a time when you are apprehensive for the peace of
the country and know not how soon the Honourable Company may
be again engaged in numerous hostilities, I should have been wanting in duty to myself and to the publick, had I not acquainted you
with this extraordinary anecdote, of which you will please to make
such use as your prudence may dictate and the public welfare
require."

A more questionable exercise of the authority of the
Government was the interposition of the members of
Council, in their capacity as Judges of the General
Court of Justice at Calcutta, to prevent Mr Bolts's
witnesses from being allowed to give evidence before
the Grand Jury on his application to the latter for
protection in May of the same year.[1] Their action

[1] See paragraphs 18 and 19 of Mr Bolts's Petition to the Directors,
pages 95 and 96.

evoked a strong protest from the members of the Grand Jury.

At a meeting of the Council held on the 15th of August a translation of a letter from " Mahomed Reza Cawn "[1] to Mr Verelst was produced, accompanied by a copy of an audacious proclamation issued by Mr Bolts, in quite a royal style, for the protection of his chief Armenian agent.

Translation of Mahomed Reza Cawn's letter :

"Coja Rafâel and Coja Estevân, two Armenians who were under the custody of Captain Harper, and sent by him to Colonel Barker, and by him delivered to Maha Rajah Seetabroy, and by Seetabroy conducted hither to me, are now at Murshedabad. Mr Bolts issues a writing in the style of a public order, or proclamation to all ranks of people ; and affixes his seal upon the face thereof, in manner of a firmann,[2] and sends it hither.

The sense of it is, that whosoever shall imprison or molest the said Armenians, shall be answerable for all Mr Bolts's balances and outstanding concerns. A copy of the writing is enclosed for your perusal, and the original is deposited with Mr Sykes. I cannot comprehend what Mr Bolts could propose by such a writing. The Armenians are both here ; consequently what Mr Bolts has written is directly levelled at the Nizam (Nabob) and the executive officers of the government acting under me ; and there never was an instance yet of any one who wrote in such a style to the Nizam and the officers of the Government."

Copy of a proclamation under Mr Bolts's hand and seal :

"BE IT KNOWN AND SIGNIFIED.—Whereas I have appointed Coja Rafâel Johanes Padry to collect my balances and outstanding debts, and to get together all my concerns in trade, which are now dispersed abroad in divers places. The aforesaid person will collect the balances from the several Assammies, according to justice and equity, and will also get together and bring away all such concerns in trade as are then outstanding on my account. Whoever, therefore, shall, without cause or pretence, impede and hinder their business, or any way molest the aforesaid person, he shall become responsible for my balances and outstanding concerns, and I will

---

[1] Muhammad Riza Ali Khan was " Naib Subah," or chief Minister.
[2] Imperial proclamation.

take due account of my affairs with him. I have written this by way of declaration."

(Signed)   WILLIAM BOLTS.

At the same meeting of the Council the Registrar attended with a protest from Mr Bolts against the intentions of the Government towards him, setting forth that

"Mr William Bolts having received positive intelligence that one Richard Smith, Colonel and Commander of the troops in the service of the Company, together with sundry other evil-minded persons then unknown, did at a certain time and place associate and hold an illegal conspiracy against the person of him, the said William Bolts, to seize and imprison him and to force him on board some ship and transport him beyond the seas—appealed to the Habeas Corpus Act for protection, and did further, for the security of his person, family, and effects against the wicked intentions of the beforesaid Richard Smith and his accessaries, present his information to the Grand Jury empanelled at the General Quarter Sessions of Oyer and Terminer held at Calcutta the twenty seventh day of May anno one thousand seven hundred and sixty eight, present Harry Verelst,. James Alexander, Claud Russell, William Aldersey, and Charles Floyer Esquires, Justices of the Peace, whereupon the said Grand Jury did proceed to take the depositions of the witnesses, but were therein prevented by the said Justices, who refused to let the witnesses be sworn upon several frivolous pretences, but particularly alledging that the witnesses were not regularly subpœnad, and expecting or pretending to expect that the Grand Jury would subpœna them,[1] whereupon the said Grand Jury did protest against the said Justices, and thereby a stop was put to the proceedings, the complaint of him, the said William Bolts being quashed, and he left without remedy. He protests against the excuses alleged as contrary to equity, custom, and truth; he has discovered, and will prove, that these gentlemen were accessaries and parties concerned with the beforesaid Richard Smith in the wicked resolution of breaking the laws in the conspiracy against him, the said William Bolts. They are members of Council, as well as Justices, and in the former capacity have committed themselves by official resolutions to this conspiracy. They are the only magistrates in Calcutta; hence he is left without his proper remedy. He believes that the illegal and malicious proceedings against him have been inspired, in some or all of these conspirators, by a jealousy and competition in trade, by resentment

---

[1] See page 76 and Mr Bolts's Petition to the Directors, pages 95 and 96.

occasioned by his efforts to obtain justice for injured persons contrary to the interests of Members of Council, and by his previous exposure of their mismanagement and misdeeds to the Court of Directors.

He therefore declares that he considers the proceedings of the said conspirators against him to be contrary to law, equity, and good conscience, and to be oppressions of the most grievous and malicious nature.

Consequently he has requested the Notary Public to make a formal protest against their proceedings to the Grand Jury, and to inform them that they and their instruments, civil, military, or naval, will be made, jointly and severally, responsible for any breach of the peace against him and for all loss or damage which may accrue to him therefrom.

The Notary Public, John Holme, accordingly presented this protest, and a copy of the official record of the proceedings at the Quarter Sessions meeting."

The Grand Jury consisted of twelve Englishmen, a good many of whom, including Mr Richard Barwell, were servants of the East India Company.

From the proceedings it appears that the first four witnesses summoned on behalf of Mr Bolts were the Sheriff, the Clerk of the Peace, and Messrs Dumbleton and Bird. As these four gentlemen were also the Secretary, Assistant Secretary, and junior assistants to the Board, the Justices, who were also Members of the Council, objected to their being called and sworn without due notice, alleging particularly in the case of the junior civilians that young and inexperienced men, who were necessarily entrusted with the knowledge of confidential proceedings and documents, might betray State secrets, if they were suddenly put into the witness-box unprepared. They also laid it down that if the Grand Jury desired to examine any witnesses, those witnesses must first be formally subpoena'd, and rebuked the Grand Jury severely for arrogating to themselves the functions of Government.[1]

This message was conveyed to the Grand Jury,

[1] See pages 95 and 96.

who shortly afterwards came into court and delivered a serious protest against the action of the Justices and a vindication of their own conduct, which is quoted in full in Mr Bolts's subsequent Petition to the Directors.

In reply to this address the Court explained more fully their objection to the abrupt summoning of Assistant and Under Secretaries, without knowing whether the inquisition related to a breach of the peace or any crime whatever, since no information therein had been laid before any Justice of the Peace or the Court. They added that if the matter under their consideration tended only to a presentment, the Court was of opinion that the information of one person, if of good character, was sufficient for them to found a presentment on.

The Jury then withdrew to reconsider their address, but returned into Court subsequently without having modified its terms.

The Court made a further remonstrance, pointing out that the Jurors' address really contained a misrepresentation of facts, since the Court had not absolutely refused to hear the witnesses, but had offered to adjourn, in order to give the Jury time to subpoena the witnesses whom they wished to examine. On enquiry from the bench, it was ascertained that no such message had been delivered to the Jury, the Juryman entrusted with the message having misunderstood the Court. Whereupon the Court desired the Jurors

"to reconsider whether they would subpoena such persons as they might think necessary and proceed to take their informations, the Court being willing, as the day was far advanced, to give them an opportunity for so doing by adjourning. The Court desire the Jurors will be assured that their attachment to the present Government is no way questioned, but on the contrary they entertain the most favourable opinion of the several members who compose the Jury; that the Jury cannot but consider that if the proceedings of the Jury this day were to become a precedent, further Juries, who it is possible may be affected with less zeal, may at pleasure under various pretences scrutinize into the most important transactions of Government, the evil consequence of which must be too apparent to need any elucidation."

This entertaining mixture of flattery and admonition, which contrasts rather abruptly with the previous rebuke, had no effect on the temper of the Jury, who "informed the Court that any farther proceedings on the matter before them were unnecessary."

At the Council meeting of the 29th of August a summons for Mr Bolts and a charge against him, on the information of the President, based on the deposition of Mr Edward Baber, were read to the Board. He was accused, with much redundant legal phraseology, of having defrauded the Board and the Company by causing his Writer to subscribe his covenant in the month of May 1765, and summoned to appear before the Board on the 5th of September to answer to the charge.

On the 5th of September Mr Bolts's reply was read to the Board:

"Sir,—After the frequent complaints and representations which I have made to the Board without being regarded or answered, the Board have no right to expect that I should attend the summons which you have just sent me by Mr James Irwin. However as the President in this single instance with respect to me has desisted from his custom of stabbing in the dark and for once dared to stand forth, I shall therefore duly attend at the time appointed and supported by conscious integrity shall I hope be able to fix the infamy where only it ought to fall."

Mr Baber then delivered in his information upon oath, and Mr Bolts having attended in consequence of the summons was called before the Board. He insisted on his accuser's being present, alleging that the expectation of seeing him was one of his principal motives for attending, and that otherwise he should not answer to any of the questions that were put to him. Mr Bolts was then desired to withdraw and the Board, debating upon the propriety of calling upon the President to appear before them, were of opinion that Mr Bolts had a legal right to require the presence of the person who had lodged the information, and accordingly sent the Secretary to request the President's attendance.

The President returned a verbal answer to the Board that he could wish they would dispense with his attendance as he imagined there was not a necessity for it since what he had alleged against Mr Bolts was only an information he had heard and not delivered as an evidence upon oath to facts of his own knowledge.

The Board still remaining in their former opinion repeated their message to the President by the Secretary, who returned for answer that he would wait on them, but soon after he sent the following letter:

"To JOHN CARTIER, ESQ., ETC. AND COUNCIL

GENTLEMEN,—Mr Baber your Secretary has acquainted me with your desire that I should attend your Board in consequence of the Information I laid before you against Mr Bolts. My knowledge of circumstances arose from the information of others, not from facts themselves. I could wish my presence to be dispensed with as there is an indelicacy if not an impropriety in my appearing as an informer before a Board of which I preside as Governor. However should you still think that my presence is absolutely necessary and my attendance at the immediate call of Mr Bolts not inconsistent— If you will adjourn the Council till the afternoon, I will attend you. This I am induced to ask from that delicacy which I think is due to my station."

In answer to which, the Board wrote him the following letter which was carried by the Secretary:

"SIR,—The whole Board felt the situation which Mr Bolts had reduced us to by obliging us to apply for your presence. We were extremely desirous of preserving the delicacy due to your station, at the same time we had our doubts of the legality of this matter. We may err, but it seems to be the opinion of the Board that every British subject has an indubitable right to have his accuser appear before him, and Mr Bolts declares he will not answer to any questions unless you are present. In this situation we are apprehensive that we shall not be able to go through the matter in question with that degree of precision which may be deemed necessary unless you favour us with your presence. And we should most readily postpone the meeting until the afternoon, but that as Mr Bolts was summoned to appear betwixt the hours of ten and twelve we conceive that as he has appeared he has answered his summons. We are extremely sorry to be so pressing on the subject, which nothing but the point of legality could authorise, and we cannot conclude this without assuring you that the respect due to you as President will ever be maintained most inviolably by this Board."

In answer to which the President repeated the desire he had expressed in his letter that the Board would adjourn until the afternoon, when he would attend them.

The Board then came to a determination of calling in Mr Bolts before them and acquainting him that if he would dispense with the absence of the President, they would immediately proceed to the business he was summoned on. But upon his refusing to comply with this proposal, he was required to attend the Board between four and five in the afternoon when the President would be present, to which he replied he would wait on them with pleasure.

"Ordered that the Secretary do wait on the Governor and request his attendance at the time appointed.

The Board met according to adjournment at $\frac{1}{2}$ after four and Mr Bolts did not attend them till $\frac{1}{2}$ hour after five, when the Information of Mr Verelst was read as also Mr Irwin's affidavit that he has served the summons on Mr William Bolts for his attendance here this day."

The information against Mr Bolts, the summons, the affidavit of Mr Irwin, and the information of Mr Baber were then successively read.

"Mr Bolts was then asked whether the information delivered was true or not? He replied that part is true and part is not true.

Q. What part is true and what is not?

A. That part is false which says Mr Bolts requested Mr Baber to permit him to execute the indenture afresh or over again and to allow him to take the said indenture home with him for that purpose. Mr Bolts further says that many of the most material circumstances seem designedly omitted and many others misrepresented which Mr Bolts will more particularly specify in his written defence which he now proposes to deliver in, previous to which Mr Bolts begs leave to remark that Mr Baber is not a competent judge having been instigated to propagate falsities solely from his having commenced a prosecution against him in the Mayor's Court (as Clerk of the Peace) for furnishing him with false records of the proceedings of the sessions of the 27th May 1768.

Mr Bolts now begs leave to read his defence.

Mr Bolts is now asked whether he has any questions to put to Mr Verelst who is now present, to which he answers he has several as will appear in the course of his defence, but which he will not now previously or detachedly ask.

Mr Verelst acquaints the Board that he knows nothing further of the matter than what is contained in the Information which he has already called on Mr Baber to support; that if Mr Bolts has any questions to put to him, if Mr Bolts pleases to commit them to writing he will answer them in the most candid manner in his power, but that he would not wish to be present when Mr Bolts enters on his defence for reasons he will assign should the Board think proper to call on him.

The President then retired having first obtained the permission of the Board, but was told that if they found it necessary from any part of Mr Bolts's defence to call on him again, they must request his attendance.

Mr Bolts begs leave in his turn to acquaint the Board that there are other circumstances relative to the matter in question, more than what is contained in the Information, with which Mr Verelst is acquainted, that to convict Mr Verelst of this it was absolutely necessary to have him present, that as Mr Verelst is permitted to go away Mr Bolts refuses to deliver or read his defence, but will transmit to the Honble. the Court of Directors to whom he will give the most honorable satisfaction.

Mr Cartier observes to Mr Bolts that it is a very singular indulgence in this Board to allow him to make so many observations on our proceedings. Mr Bolts begs leave to observe that it is a very singular condescension in him to have attended upon the summons he has received to answer to what the Board would willingly deem a misdemeanour, which if it was so, the present Board have no right to take cognizance of.

Mr Bolts being again asked if he chuses to make his defence, he declares he will not unless Mr Verelst is present.

F

Mr Bolts is ordered to retire.

The Board taking the whole proceedings into consideration, and remarking that Mr Bolts has repeatedly refused making any defence unless Mr Verelst was present which was judged by no means necessary since he (Mr Verelst) had attended while the Information and evidence were read and had acquainted the Board he would be ready to attend again whenever they had any question to put to him.

They are of opinion that Mr Bolts has by no means acquitted himself of the charge brought against him, but on the contrary in part acknowledged it. They therefore deem him an improper person to be a member of a Court of Justice, and by virtue of the power vested in them by the royal charter granted them in the twenty-sixth year of the reign of King George the Second, they accordingly disqualify him from being any longer an Alderman of the Honble. the Mayor's Court, of which it is agreed to advise the Court by the following letter from the Secretary:

'To the Honourable the Mayor's Court of Calcutta

Gentlemen,—The Honble. the President and Council, having by virtue of the royal charter granted in the twenty-sixth year of the reign of our Sovereign Lord George the Second for reasonable cause thought proper to remove Mr William Bolts from sitting as an Alderman in your Court, I have it in command from them to acquaint you that he is accordingly removed and his seat vacated.'[1]

The Board think it necessary to remark that whatever appears as said by Mr Bolts was taken verbatim from his own mouth, and that whilst the Assistant Secretary copied it, he also copied it in a memorandum book and compared it with the proceedings."

On the 13th of September Mr Bolts's letter in reply to the charge was received, together with one addressed to the Court of Directors.[2]

According to the promise, which he personally made on the 5th instant, upon their dispensing with his accuser's attendance at the enquiry then on foot, he

[1] On this occasion, in spite of the undoubted illegality of the method of Mr Bolts's removal, the Mayor's Court was all complaisance, and signified in a letter dated the 13th of September that Mr Bolts's seat as an Alderman was vacated ; the Board were also requested to appoint another person to serve in his stead. The request was promptly met by the Board's appointment of a Mr James Lawrell to serve as Alderman instead of Mr Bolts.

[2] See below, page 93, etc.

herewith sends the papers which he then had prepared and in his pocket in answer to the many groundless accusations recorded upon their consultations, by which they had endeavoured to injure him.

The stop put to the enquiry on Mr Verelst's information, in consequence of his non-attendance, has deprived him of the advantage he had proposed to himself of producing his witnesses and vouchers to convict that gentleman personally of his falsity, in the face of the whole Board. He has therefore been obliged to have recourse to affidavits made in the Mayor's Court, of which one original and two copies are annexed to the accompanying papers for transmission to the Court of Directors by the *Valentine*, Captain Purvis. An original Bengal letter referred to in his papers likewise goes enclosed, as he has been deprived of the opportunity of delivering it to Mr Verelst personally before the Board; and his address to the Board containing his justification, which, though enclosed for despatch to the Court of Directors, should also be regarded as a separate address to the Board and be carefully perused.

Their proceedings of the 5th instant speak for themselves,

"as well from the malice and partiality apparent in the written proceedings as from the huggermugger method pursued in the enquiry with shut doors by you Gentlemen, the Inquisitors, who though sitting as my pretended judges, were in fact no other than what you have of long been, parties concerned and self-interested in the accusing and oppressing of me. The publick will, I flatter myself, espouse my cause and justify me; it may be happy for you Gentlemen if you can stand that test with respect to your own conduct, on which I have not had time to say half what I have in store.

As to you Gentlemen presuming to the authority of removing me from my seat as an alderman in the Honble. the Mayor's Court, it is an error into which you have been led by your Counsellor, and which does not merit my notice. I shall therefore only remark that whatever steps may be taken in consequence of your said Resolutions, I do hereby protest against every person concerned therein, and shall not fail to make them answerable for the severest damages.

I shall pursue my former method of sending home copies of all papers attested in the Mayor's Court for fear of miscarriage."

This letter was ordered to be entered on the records, and his letter to the Directors was ordered to be transmitted to them.

"As Mr Bolts has particularly made a very libellous attack on the character of the President in his letter to the Court of Directors,

Mr Verelst desires it may be recorded that he solemnly declares every assertion contained in Mr Bolts's letter to the Honble. the Court of Directors which tends to reflect on his character is infamously scandalous and false, that he shall particularly answer Mr Bolts's accusation, when more at leisure as he cannot do it at present without retarding the dispatch of the ship."

The Council then proceeded to record the Resolution reproduced on pages 85 and 86.

The Council had at last made up their minds to proceed to extremities, and had ordered Captain Purvis to detain his ship, the *Valentine*, in order that Mr Bolts might be conveyed home in her as a prisoner. Mr Bolts having got wind of their design threatened Captain Purvis with legal proceedings against him in England, should he comply with the Council's mandate ; and on the 6th of September the latter made a formal protest through the public notary against the detention of the *-Valentine*, contrary to the terms of the charter party. He also objected to taking Mr Bolts on board his vessel, unless he were given a bond of indemnification. He even pressed at first for separate bonds of indemnification from each individual member of the Council, though he seems to have afterwards waived the latter demand.[1]

A few days later Mr Bolts, being anxious to take

[1] The *Valentine* had been an unlucky ship, as she had run aground between Gravesend and the Downs on the outward voyage, and did not reach Calcutta till the 6th of June. Captain Purvis was, perhaps, apprehensive of further discomfiture, with such a "sea-lawyer" as Mr Bolts on board.

the public of Calcutta into his confidence, and to stir
up the European community against the Government,
had recourse to an extraordinary expedient for publishing certain manuscript information which he had in
his possession. He affixed to the door of the Council
House at Calcutta a proclamation inviting the public
to repair to his house between certain hours, in order
to read or take copies of his manuscripts. The
incident is interesting as illustrating the curious fact
that there was as yet no printing press in Calcutta,
and is quoted by Mr Busteed in his delightful
"Echoes from old Calcutta" in this sense.

"To The Public

Mr Bolts takes this method of informing the public, that the
want of a printing press in this city being of great disadvantage in
business, and making it extremely difficult to communicate such
intelligence to the community as is of the utmost importance to
every British subject, he is ready to give the best encouragement
to any person or persons who are versed in the business of printing,
and will undertake to manage a press, the types and utensils of
which he can produce.

In the meantime he begs leave to inform the public, that having
in manuscript many things to communicate, which most intimately
concern every individual, any person who may be induced by
curiosity or other laudable motives, will be permitted at Mr Bolts's
house, to read or take copies of the same; a person will give due
attendance at the house from ten to twelve every morning."

This seems to have been the last straw. On the
13th of September the Council met and recorded the
following "minute against Mr William Bolts":

"Mr William Bolts having obstinately refused complying with
our frequent and repeated orders to return to England, having
persisted to insult our authority and Government and to subvert
the principles of subordination—having aggravated every circumstance of his conduct which is so strongly pointed out and
represented in our consultation of the 4th November 1767, and
which then made us deem it necessary for the support of our
authority and for the preservation of the peace order and tranquility
of this settlement and throughout the Company's possessions in

Bengal—to resolve on seizing his person and forcibly sending him home, it became more particularly incumbent on the Board to enforce these orders, and accordingly it was agreed and resolved to send Mr Bolts home a prisoner on board the *Valentine*—and Captain J. Purvis having represented to the President some doubts how far he may be made responsible for the execution of such a measure, Mr Bolts having already served Captain Purvis with a protest against his taking him on board the *Valentine*, the Board in order to remove every apprehension which Captain Purvis seems to entertain of the consequence of receiving him, they do further agree as the agents and representatives of the Company to give Captain Purvis an indemnification for his satisfaction,[1] and from that consideration only, as they are well convinced of the legality of such a measure from several Acts of Parliament, and that it will meet with the approbation of the Honourable Court of Directors, as well as those similar measures which were taken in the year 1766 with regard to the officers who resigned,[2] and were sent home."

On the same date they devoted twelve paragraphs of their letter to the Court of Directors to a narrative of Mr Bolts's misdoings and a vindication of the contemplated expulsion.

Having referred to their repeated orders to Mr Bolts to repair to England, to his insolent defiance,

---

[1] A copy of this bond is entered on the minutes of Consultations for the 19th of September 1768. It sets forth, with the usual verbiage, that the members of the Bengal Council bind themselves by name, as agents of the East India Company, in the sum of 50,000*l.* to Captain John Purvis, to indemnify him and his heirs for any loss or damage that may accrue to him through receiving Mr Bolts on board his ship ; also that the Council have found it necessary to order and direct, and have accordingly ordered and directed Mr William Bolts to be seized and carried on board the *Valentine* for conveyance to England. The reasons given for the order are Mr Bolts's disregard of and disobedience to the repeated orders of the Council to quit Bengal, and his openly acknowledged and even vaunted persistence in "a very large and extensive trade throughout all India . . . in open defiance and violation of the several statutes in that case made and provided," besides the necessity of making an example " pour encourager les autres."

That Captain Purvis was well advised in seeking to secure himself in advance against Mr Bolts's vengeance, is apparent from a letter of his, read to the Court of Directors on the 12th of June, 1772, in which he desires the Court would defend him in a prosecution commenced against him by Mr Bolts. The Court agreed to do so.

[2] Referring to the conspiracy of the officers of the Company's army in India to compel Lord Clive to withdraw his prohibition of double field allowance by a general resignation of their commissions.

and to their refusal to take any further notice of his protests and letters, they drew particular attention to his dealings with Mr Fenwick and Mr Baber, and to the notorious letter to Muhammad Riza Ali Khan.

" Mr Fenwick, one of your junior servants, was connected with Mr Bolts. This young man was employed in your Secretary's office, and so far forgot his duty to his employers that he gave Mr Bolts a copy of a minute delivered in by Colonel Smith, the 18th May. We leave you . . . to judge what arguments and persuasions must have been made use of to prevail on this inexperienced youth to be guilty of such notorious breach of trust, and you will doubtless at the same time perceive that the inevitable ruin of this young man's prospects in life was no consideration, when put in competition with the accomplishment of Mr Bolts's views.

This minute Mr Bolts layed before our Grand Jury at our Quarter Sessions, and prepared an address upon the occasion which is entered in our consultations of the 30th May.

Though much may be urged in defence of youth when attacked by the solicitations of an artful and designing man, yet so flagrant a breach of duty, . . . We dismissed Mr Fenwick your service. . . .[1] We must now lay before you a circumstance which merits your particular attention, as it appears to us to be of such nature that we think it ought to terminate in a court of justice. The President acquainted us that Mr Baber, when sub-secretary, had reported to him that Mr Bolts, instead of duly executing the covenants you sent out prohibiting your servants receiving presents, did elude your orders, and instead of subscribing to them himself employed a writer to sign his name for him. This circumstance came to Mr Baber's knowledge from Mr Bolts endeavouring . . . to persuade him to be guilty of a breach of his duty and to deliver up the covenants to him which are entrusted to his charge, that he might execute them over again. The President laying this before us, we called on Mr Baber to relate all he knew of the matter, and

---

[1] Poor Mr Fenwick had made a vain appeal to the Governor for forgiveness, dated the 26th of May, on the rather weak grounds, first, that he was and still is ignorant of the "*ingrediousness*" (sic) of his fault, and secondly, that he "had not particularly observed the order stuck up in the outer room of the Council House," and thirdly, that it was his first offence. Subsequently, however, the Board relented, on a second representation from Mr Fenwick, so far as to permit him to remain in India till the Directors' pleasure could be known. In their despatch of the 23rd of March 1770 the Directors, in consideration of his youth and the Board's representation, readmitted him to the service and ordered the Board to reprimand him severely for his late imprudent conduct.

we beg leave to refer you to his declaration on oath entered on Consultation 5th September for the particulars.

From this relation it appears that Mr Bolts was very sensible of the unjustifiable step he had taken, and was very earnest and solicitous to prevent the consequences of it by the method he took to prevail on the sub-secretary to get the covenants out of his hands. A regular enquiry was made into the matter, as appears upon our consults of the 5th instant, for the particulars.

You will observe from the date of this letter of Mr Bolts, it was laid before us too late to be particularly replied to by this ship, but we shall not fail answering it very fully in our next advices. In the meantime, however, the President desired it might be recorded, as his character is particularly reflected upon, that he solemnly declares every assertion contained in Mr Bolts's letter to the Honourable Court of Directors which tends to reflect on his character, is infamously scandalous and false, that he shall particularly answer to Mr Bolts's accusation when more at leisure, as he cannot do it at present without retarding the despatch of the ship.

A very particular and . . . a most unparalleled instance of Mr Bolts's insolence, the defiance he bids to both your and our orders, and the contempt with which he treats the Government, is fully exemplified in a letter he took on him to write to Mahomed Reza Cawn, and which is entered in our consultation of the 15th August. He has here assumed a privilege you have vested in your president only, and he has here dared to dictate in the most imperious and insolent style to one of the ministers of the Government.

Such, gentlemen, has been the conduct of Mr Bolts, and there are many other circumstances which for want of time we must defer unto the next ship. That a man who has thus trampled upon the authority of the Government, who has violated his fidelity to his employers, who has endeavoured to seduce your servants from their duty, and who has in multiplied instances proved himself unworthy of the Company's protection, should be compelled to quit the settlement, admits not of a moment's doubt, and confident that you . . . will see the necessity of this measure which is taken for the support of Government in the same light you did that taken in 1766 with regard to the officers, we assure ourselves the resolution we have taken of sending Mr Bolts home will also meet with your approbation, since we consider it absolutely necessary to the peace order and tranquillity of your settlement and throughout the Company's possessions in Bengal.

We should not have deferred so long carrying into execution our resolution of the 5th November 1767, but having wrote you very fully concerning the refractory behaviour of Messrs Duffield and Robertson, and requesting you in a very earnest and particular manner to inform us of the extent of our authority to be used in similar cases, we expected by this year's shipping to have received very ample instructions for our future conduct on so important a point. However the approbation you have expressed at the measures pursued for sending home those officers have determined us to come to the foregoing resolution with regard to Mr Bolts."

(The long expected pronouncement of the Directors on the question whether the Council were authorised to compel Mr Bolts to leave India was not penned until the 11th of November 1768, after the expulsion had been effected :

"Mr Bolts has been a very unworthy and unprofitable servant to the Company, his conduct has been distinguished by a tenacious adherence to those pernicious principles relative to the rights to the inland trade, in which he appears to have been so conspicuously oppressive—by repeated instances of disobedience to the orders of his superiors abroad—and above all by the basest ingratitude to the Company under whom he had acquired an ample fortune, in exposing their secrets to Mr Gentil at Sujah Dowlah's Court and to his agents at other Indostan Courts, which we look upon in the light of a high crime and misdemeanour. Under these circumstances you were warranted in pursuing the most speedy and effectual measures for freeing the country of so dangerous a member of Society, and we therefore approve of your obliging him to repair to Europe by the first opportunity, which if not already done must be carried into execution by the first ship."

In a later paragraph of the same letter there is reference to Mr Bolts's letter to the Directors, "relative to the difficulty of obtaining goods equal to our demands and the disputes with the foreign Companies thereon.")

POSTSCRIPT TO THE ABOVE LETTER, DATED THE 19TH SEPTEMBER 1768

"Captain Purvis being called before the Board and acquainted with our design to send Mr Bolts to Europe on board his ship by force, if he would not embark without it, Captain Purvis urged many doubts concerning the legality of his receiving Mr Bolts on board the *Valentine*, when sent against his own consent, in justice to him we did not hesitate as your agents to offer him a bond of indemnification. . . . To our great surprise he did not think such a bond a sufficient indemnification, doubting how far the Company would in this case acknowledge the acts of their agents. He requested from us as individuals separate bonds of indemnification. So convinced are we of the necessity of sending this dangerous man out of the settlement, that we should not have hesitated granting him even this extraordinary request, but we could not consent to make that a private act which we judge ourselves authorised to carry into execution by virtue of Acts of Parliament, and as it would also give the litigious man a pretence to arraign our conduct as proceeding from motives of private resentment instead of public utility. If we entertained a moment's doubt but that you would support your servants in all acts which they undertake for the better administration of your affairs, we should on this occasion point out the necessity of indemnifying Captain Purvis. This case you must consider will stand as a precedent to all future time, and if this act does not meet with your steady support, it is impossible your administration should ever have it in their power to send home any person whatever, though you yourselves have lately had occasion to enforce the execution of such measures.

As a corroborative proof of what we have alleged concerning the turbulent character of Mr Bolts and his factious attempts to sow the seeds of discontent in the settlement, we have sent you a copy of a paper which was affixed upon the door of the Council House and at several other public places. This was seen by many persons in the settlement, amongst others some of your servants, whose declaration upon oath before the Mayor of their having seen such a paper makes a number in the packet."

CHAPTER XIV

MR BOLTS'S DEPORTATION AND HIS PETITION TO THE DIRECTORS

ON Friday the 23rd of September the bolt fell. Under orders from the Council, Captain Robert Coxe,[1] with a guard of sepoys, proceeded to Mr Bolts's house, and having surrounded it, made him a prisoner and carried him off to the schooner *Cuddalore*, from which he was transferred six days later to the *Valentine*. The latter vessel sailed on the 30th of September, was reported out at sea on the 3rd of October, and reached Plymouth on the 30th of April 1769, after a seven months' voyage, an unusually long one even at that period.

Mr Bolts appears to have fared sumptuously on board the *Valentine*, for in January of the following year the Directors note :

"We have paid Captain Purvis one hundred guineas for the passage of Mr Bolts, who you sent home on the *Valentine*, upon the Captain's representing that he was put to an extraordinary expense on Mr Bolts's account and had not received any consideration for the same."

The report of Captain Coxe to the Council, written on the day of the seizure, says that finding the doors of Mr Bolts's house open he went upstairs, and found Mr Bolts alone, and showing him the Board's order

---

[1] Captain Coxe afterwards had to appear as a witness in the suit instituted by Mr Bolts in consequence of this seizure. The Directors gave him a present of 100*l.* for his expenses and trouble in the matter, and an advance of 200*l.*—repayable—to enable him to return to Bengal. He was a Bombay officer brought to Bengal owing to the Mutiny of 1766.

Mr Bolts said he would not leave his house unless Captain Coxe made him a prisoner and forced him; the Captain telling him he was glad to find him so well prepared to leave the place, he said he had expected he should be forced away, and had been very busy in getting himself in readiness. After this Captain Coxe, thinking he had made a very unnecessary delay, and fearing he intended to procure himself to be arrested for debt, desired him to make dispatch, upon which he again said he would not go unless Captain Coxe forced him. Whereupon the Captain called two sepoys, who put their hands on his shoulder by his own desire, saying he would not go if they did not take hold of him; he then came downstairs, desiring some gentlemen present to take notice that he was forced out of his own house. Captain Coxe adds that Mr Bolts was, in every respect, prepared for this order, having his books and papers prepared in great form, which he delivered to his attornies, telling them that everything was so plain they could not make a mistake, observing that plain directions were given as to such debts as they were to get in.

In their second postcript to the letter of the 13th of September, dated the 24th of September, the Board wrote:

"We beg leave to add a circumstance relative to Mr Bolts that has happened since closing our despatches. We informed you in our letter we had directed him to be sent by force to England, if he refused to comply with our orders, as we imagined he did refuse to comply with them, and Captain Robert Coxe was ordered to seize him with a guard and carry him on board the *Cuddalore* schooner, which was prepared to receive him and his necessaries; but he was particularly cautioned that in performing this service he should force no doors, locks, or windows, and use as little violence as the nature of the case would admit. Mr Bolts has been accordingly conducted under a guard on board the *Cuddalore* schooner, and is now proceeding to be embarked on board the *Valentine* in order to be sent to England, and we must beg leave to observe to you, gentlemen, that it appears from the whole tenor of his conduct that his aim has been to reduce us to the necessity of taking this measure. He had prepared himself for the voyage and had, we are informed, all and every necessary ready in order to embark when he was seized by Captain Coxe."

Mr Bolts's own account of the seizure and of the events that led up to it, is contained in the petition to the Directors which he sent in a fortnight after his arrival in London. It is preceded by a brief sketch of his career in the Company's service.

The Petition of William Bolts late of Bengal to the Court of Directors sets forth :

"(1) That he entered the Company's service in 1759, and served it diligently and faithfully till he resigned on the 10th November 1766.

(2) That he resigned on account of 'the confusion and injustice which prevailed after the appointment of the Select Committee, all gradations of rank and service being set at nought, and every preferment to every office being disposed of from faction, private interest, and party, without any regard to merit and service,' etc. (*i.e.* because he had been passed over for promotion in favour of Mr John Graham and Mr Isaac Sage, his juniors in the service).

(3) That after his resignation he continued to prosecute his concerns as a merchant and attorney to retired civilians or merchants, and also as an Alderman, or one of the Judges of the Mayor's Court of Calcutta, an honour bestowed on him some time before his resignation.

(4) That the Governor and Council 'having formed several cruel, unjust, and oppressive monopolies,' particularly in cotton, salt, betel-nut, piece goods, saltpetre, and opium, 'contrary to natural justice and the express orders of the Honourable Court of Directors repeated again and again, it was his misfortune in the prosecution of his affairs to clash with their interests; that he thereby incurred their heavy resentment, particularly that of Governor Verelst and Colonel Richard Smith, which they vented by acts of the greatest cruelty and injustice against him.'

(5) That the Governor and the Select Committee banished him from Bengal by an order issued on the 20th April 1767, in accordance with a sentence of the Committee dated the 18th April, when he had been, though a British subject and judge of the Mayor's Court, condemned to the severest

punishment short of death, 'unacquainted with his charge, unconfronted with his accusers, unheard in his defence.'

(6) That the sentence of banishment was absurd and inconsistent, he being condemned 'for what the Committee supposed he would committ,'[1] and that he denies every part of the accusation contained in it.

(7) That, apart from the protection which every British subject has a right to claim, he was a Judge of the Mayor's Court, under the protection of the charter of the 26th, George II —irremovable 'unless upon a complaint in writing first exhibited against him, and that he have a reasonable time given him to make his defence,' none of which requisites were complied with in his case.

(8) That in defiance of this guarantee the Governor and Council directed the Mayor's Court to remove him from his seat as a Judge of that Court.

(9) That the Mayor's Court replied 'that when a vacancy of an Alderman shall happen in the Mayor's Court, the Governor and Council shall be acquainted therewith.'

(10) That to avoid the seizure of his person, which he was informed the Governor and Council contemplated in conformity with the sentence of banishment, he was obliged to withdraw from Calcutta to Chinsurah, to attend to the settlement of his affairs.

(11) That the Governor and Council maliciously ordered his agents and gomastahs employed in collecting his outstanding concerns to be seized and imprisoned, whereby he and his constituents suffered heavy loss, while his servants and the manufacturers from whom he was receiving the balances due on contracts 'were taken and employed by sundry members of the Council, who availed themselves of this wicked act to establish their own trade upon the ruin of the petitioner.'

(12) That his agents—reputable Armenian Christians—had not been guilty of any breach of the laws of the country nor acted against the interests of the Company; nevertheless they were suddenly seized and imprisoned 'without either they or your petitioner being acquainted with any reason for such imprisonment.'

(13) That he thereupon returned to Calcutta and wrote various letters claiming redress as a British subject from the Governor and Council.

(14) That no attention was paid to his remonstrances or to his agents' petitions and those of 'their distressed parents and

---

[1] *Cf.* page 49, note.

wives,' but that they were kept in prison for five months; then the Governor and Council suddenly released them 'without ever having accused, confronted, or heard them'. . . 'even refusing them perwannahs or dustucks to enable them to bring down their effects' from up country.

(15) That Govenor Verelst wrote to him in March 1768, that he had given no orders to impede his business: 'I know of no orders for impeding the business of your gomastahs in particular in the dominions of Suja Dowlah and Bulwansingh."

(16) That this assertion was confirmed by a letter from the Secretary to the Select Committee by order of the Board in April 1768, both originals being in petitioner's possession.

(17) But nevertheless the Governor in 1767 wrote the following minute: 'The President is further informed that Mr Bolts has an Armenian agent in Fysabad named Cogee Rafael, another at Banaras named Cogee Melcomb, and a third residing near Ghazipore, by name Cogee Gregory; through these people he ungratefully endeavours to injure the interests of those in whose service he has raised an independency, and those Armenians under the character of English gomastahs are striving to establish themselves in Sujah Dowlah's dominions upon the footing they were formerly at Muxadabad, notwithstanding the Nabob on account of some malpractices has lately forbidden them his presence. The President and Council has however desired His Excellency to banish all such as are in his country under the pretexts of being gomastahs to the English.'

(18) That your Petitioner being also himself threatened with violence, and finding no reddress could be had from the said Governor and Council, who had thus violated every principle of private honour and publick justice, did apply for the protection of the General Court of Justice at Calcutta, and did accordingly prefer his complaint to the Grand Jury,[1] when by an extraordinary interposition of the said Governor and Council then sitting as judges the different evidences in the cause were, on the most frivolous and unheard of pretexts, refused by the Court to be sworn or admitted to appear before the Grand Jury; though such evidences were present in Court and demanded both by the jury and the prosecutor.

---

[1] See Appendix.

(19) That in consequence thereof the Grand Jury of the Country did deliver into Court the following protest, which was the occasion of the breaking up of the Court and thereby obstructing the whole course of public justice in the settlement, viz :—

'The Grand Jury impanelled and sworn at Quarter Sessions held this 27th day of May 1768 in the town of Calcutta take this method to acquaint the Honourable Justices of the Peace now sitting that an information has been laid before them on oath by William Bolts, inhabitant of Calcutta, whereupon the Grand Jury summoned the witnesses named in the information in order to being examined, one of whom being the Sheriff and the other the Clerk of the Peace, the Bench of Justices thought proper to refuse their attendance on the Grand Jury, whereupon other witnesses were summoned by an officer of the Court, as the Grand Jury conceive in the usual manner, which the Bench of Justices were pleased to disapprove of, as the Grand Jury understood by a message from the Bench delivered to them by Mr George Lear one of their body; who also delivered further that the Bench were of opinion that the Grand Jury seemed to aim at assuming a power superior to the Government. The Grand Jury are deeply concerned to find that their endeavours to acquit themselves of their duty as bound by their oaths should have brought upon them so severe a reflection from the Bench which they are not conscious of having deserved, and they will venture to say that no Grand Jury was ever better disposed to the Government than the present.   In case the Bench do persevere in their resolution of not permitting the Grand Jury to examine witnesses upon oath touching the said information and refuse to swear in such witnesses, the Grand Jury have no other method of proceeding left (as without the examination of witnesses they cannot collect the opinions of the jurors) but to deliver in the said information to the Bench of Justices, with this address, who will be answerable for all consequences.   (Signed)   CORNELIUS GODWIN, *Foreman.*'

(20) That soon after this[1] your Petitioner's house was surrounded and himself seized by a military force, and being allowed only about two hours to pack up his clothes was dragged from his family on board a schooner under close confinement, where he was kept six days and nights under the guard of the said soldiers with drawn bayonets, and from thence conveyed on board the *Valentine* bound for England, then under sail, in order to be brought a prisoner to England.

---

[1] A very inaccurate statement.   It was nearly four months later, viz., on the 23rd of September.

(21) "That by such cruel and illegal proceedings the principal part of your Petitioner's fortune, the fruits of the toil of many years, as well as the fortunes of many persons for whom he was attorney, to the amount altogether of upwards of one hundred and ten thousand pounds sterling, are left at the mercy of the natives in different parts of the country, the greatest part of which he reasonably presumes under the oppressions he has suffered will never be recovered without the immediate interposition of the Court of -Directors."

(22) "That your Petitioner on board the ship *Valentine* arrived at Plymouth the 30th April pass'd, and now appears before the present Court of Directors claiming such relief as they may think his case deserves, being desirous and willing to answer to any part of his conduct which may appear to require justification, and in particular humbly requesting to be informed whether the proceedings of the said Honourable Company's Governor and Council in Bengal towards your Petitioner are vindicated or condemned by this Honourable Court. And your Petitioner as in duty bound shall ever pray.

(Signed)   WILLIAM BOLTS."[1]

London. The 19th May 1769.

The refusal of the Council to pay any attention to Mr Bolts's demands for redress for the seizure and imprisonment without trial of his Armenian agents proved to have been impolitic, for at Mr Bolts's instigation and, doubtless, at his expense, three of them followed him to London, to the intense annoyance of the Directors. In their letter to the Council of the 23rd of January 1770 they give vent to their displeasure in very plain language :

"Cogee Gregore, Coja Maul, and Cogee Johannes Padre Raphael, Armenian merchants, have presented a memorial to us complaining that they had been seized, imprisoned, and sent down from Sujah Dowlah and Bulwant Singh's countryes (where they resided with the consent of those princes) to Patna and Meerchidabad, and that they continued under confinement a long while and suffered other hardships and indignities, to the great detriment of their affairs, and

---

[1] The Petition was considered by the Court of Directors and referred to the Joint Committee of Correspondence and Lawsuits at the meeting of the 20th May 1769.

G

notwithstanding they several times applied to your President to know the reasons for such ill-treatment, yet they could not learn the cause or procure any redress, and therefore have been obliged to come to England in order to seek that justice they were denied in Bengal, and requesting we would make good their losses or order home President Verelst and such other servants as shall appear to have been the acting persons in those oppressions. We enclose copy of their memorial, and expect a faithful relation of the whole affair, with your motives, that we may do them justice for any injuries it shall appear they have sustained, tho' we hope the allegations in their memorial are not well founded. You should have endeavoured to have accommodated this affair in Bengal, as their appearance here in this clamorous manner may prove prejudicial to our affairs and is very unpleasing."

In their Letter to Court of the 2nd of April 1771 the Board explained their expulsion of the Armenian gomastahs as due to the discovery that the latter were intriguing at the Court of Shuja-u-Daula, and were believed on good grounds to have given Mr Bolts copies of the Board's correspondence with the Vizier. The actions of the Vizier had caused mistrust; affairs were critical, it was necessary to stop the intrigues at all hazards, Mr Bolts was insolently defying the orders prohibiting the residence of the gomastahs of English gentlemen in the territories of Shuja-u-Daula and Bulwant Singh, and his agents were entering on new business; their motives were purely political, not personal.

CHAPTER XV

THE RIGHT OF EXPULSION

THE long delay in Mr Bolts's case before recourse
was had to forcible expulsion was due partly to
the uncertainty of the Council whether they could
count upon the support of the Directors if they resorted to physical force, partly to the doubts of the
legality of seizure and deportation in the case of an
ex-civil servant, doubts which may have been present
to the minds of the Council, though they affected to
feel none, and which were certainly entertained at
first by the Court of Directors. Apart from the
recent case of the expulsion of the mutinous officers
who vainly attempted to intimidate Lord Clive, there
had been some previous instances in which the
Directors had sanctioned a resort to forcible expulsion.

In March 1757 we find them writing in the following terms regarding the case of Captain Durand to the
Council at Fort William [1]:

"At the same time we cannot avoid taking notice of the insolent
behaviour of Captain Durand as tending to such a contempt for our
authority as ought never to be borne. Your denying him therefore
the Company's protection was a very proper measure, more especially
as we know of no license he has ever had to reside in any place in
India. . . . If Captain Durand continues to misbehave, you have
our direction for sending him home immediately; as you are likewise any other person or persons who shall be guilty of any kind of
insolent behaviour and contempt of your authority."

---

[1] Holwell, soon afterwards the hero of the defence of Calcutta and of
the Black Hole, had proposed to give Captain Durand twenty-four hours'
notice to leave for England, though he had large business concerns in
Bengal.

Similar directions were given in the case of one Dumbleton, an attorney. Other precedents were furnished by the case of Mr Douglas (Consults, January 6th, 1758) and of a pilot named Toole of whom the Council wrote—in December 1759: "being of a troublesome and refractory behaviour, we ordered him to prepare to return to Europe by one of the first ships of the season." A number of cases put to famous counsel mostly in the years 1756 and 1757, among whom were John Dunning, counsel for Wilkes, afterwards Lord Ashburton, and William Murray, afterwards Lord Mansfield, are quoted in Mr Bolts's "Considerations."

It was not, however, till October 1767 that the Directors got from Mr Charles Sayer an opinion on which they thought they might safely act. He replied to the questions stated for his opinion :

(1) "That if ex-civilians were seized and sent home, they would, upon an action brought for such force, recover damages too trivial for the Company to regard," and

(2) "That an Act rendering liable to seizure and deportation all ex-civilians who should trade or be found within the Company's limits in India without their license and authority, might be easily obtained from Parliament, almost without debate, as the penalties had been already approved by Parliament in the case of free merchants, and the persons whom it was now desired to include—viz. ex-civilians— were fully within the description of 'trading or being found in India without the Company's license.'"

An attempt was made by the Directors in March 1770 through their Chairman to carry out the latter suggestion. A Bill was submitted to Parliament entitled a "Bill for compelling persons dismissed the service of the East India Company, to depart from the East Indies, and for better regulating the servants of the said Company"; but the attempt to secure the passing of the Bill failed.

Nevertheless we find them writing to the Council in April 1771:

"In order to determine your powers for sending home persons who may have infringed the rights of the Company or acted in defiance of the authority vested by us in our servants, we herewith transmit in duplicate to our President and Council a particular power or commission under the Company's seal for that purpose; and as you will thereby see how far our servants are justified in seizing and sending to England any of his Majesty's subjects who may violate the rights and privileges granted to the Company by various Acts of Parliament, we refer you to the same for your guidance."

Thirteen years later the powers of the Government remain still obscure and ill-defined. In 1781 a reference was made by the Governor-General and Council of the following two points to the Advocate-General:

(1) "Whether an officer who had been dismissed the army by sentence of a Court Martial might, under any of the Acts of Parliament which empowered the Company to seize and send home unlicensed persons and delinquents, be seized and sent home?"

(2) "Whether the Governor-General and Council might legally seize and send home all such persons as should be dismissed the service by the authority of Government or by sentence of a Court Martial?"

The Advocate-General gave it as his opinion that all persons so circumstanced were equally beyond the reach of the Acts referred to, and strongly recommended an application to Parliament for more extensive powers of dealing with such cases.

The reference arose from the case of one Donnelly, who having been dismissed the army by sentence of a Court Martial, was seized and sent home by executive order dated the 29th January 1781 under the signatures of Warren Hastings and Wheeler.

In 1784 it was agreed to send the Advocate-General's opinion to the Directors and press for further legislation on the right of seizure and deportation.

CHAPTER XVI

THE DIRECTORS ON MR BOLTS'S EXPULSION

ON the whole question of the expulsion of Mr Bolts the Directors expressed their opinion at considerable length in a despatch dated the 23rd of March 1770:

"The complaints of Mr William Bolts to us and his appeals to the public against the President and Council of Calcutta and also the Select Committee there are of too serious and interesting a nature not to deserve our particular attention and consideration.

We have ordered a full state of his case and every material circumstance attending it, collected from the different accounts and papers we have been furnished with (except what regarded his Armenian merchants who are now in London and of whom we shall hereafter make mention) to be laid before the most eminent Council in this country, as well as the Company's standing Council, and we shall now communicate to you the substance of their concurrent opinions upon different points respecting his affair, as well as our directions for the future regulation of your conduct in matters of the like nature.

By an Act of Parliament 9th George the First a covenanted servant who has been dismissed or who has resigned may have notice given him to quit India in case he is not otherwise lawfully authorised to continue there. And if such person shall refuse to depart from the East Indies after reasonable time allowed (12 months in ordinary cases seems very sufficient) for settling his accounts and calling in his effects, he will be liable to be seized and brought to England and prosecuted as an offender according to the provisions of that statute. But this power ought to be very tenderly exercised in all cases and only for the sake of public good, where the priviledges and commerce of the Company are invaded by such offenders, their regulations violated, and their European or Indian enemies abetted and supported.

In the present case the President and Council appear from the papers to have had just grounds of dissatisfaction with Mr Bolts, but they have given him considerable advantages against themselves in the course of their proceedings.

First—the appointment of him to the office of Alderman after the letter of suspension of August 1766 amounts in law to a license to remain in India (tho' not to trade there) the very nature of his duties and office under the charter of establishing Courts of Justice in Bengal requiring his acceptance of the office and his attendance under penalties. The consequence of this is that every notice to depart subsequent to his nomination as an Alderman till after a legal removal from that office may be considered as void in law, being given to a person not 'found or being in the East Indies without license' but (as the above mentioned statute 9th George the First expresses it) 'lawfully authorised thereunto.' The office of Alderman continues for life and can be vacanted only by voluntary departure or by a motion for reasonable cause in the judicial manner required by the charter. Therefore an Alderman is less dependent on the discretionary powers of the President and Council than a free merchant whose license is expired, or a mere servant who is dismissed or has resigned. It is not improbable that Mr Bolts resigned the service of the Company in November 1766 in order to avail himself of the benefit of this distinction.

Secondly—it is doubtful whether Mr Bolts has been duly and legally removed from his office of Alderman. As to the offence charged upon him in endeavouring to secrete and suppress or render ineffectual his indentures with the Company for the sake of defeating any action for breach of the covenant, it seems clear that (by reason of the relation which the different branches of the Company's service bear to each other and to the whole of their constitution) a misbehaviour or misdemeanour as described might be the foundation of a complaint against him in his corporate capacity, and if fully charged and proved, be a reasonable cause of amotion. But tappears that no steps were taken for that purpose from November 1766 when he resigned till long after the notice to depart and the peremptory order of May 4th 1768 that he should be sent to Europe by the first ship dispatch'd that season. The information against him was not exhibited till the end of August 1768 within less than a month of his seizure,[1] not so much by way of original complaint seemingly as by way of recrimination to retaliate for his presentment to the Grand Jury and his several protests and prosecution of Baber and Broughton, the Clerk of the Peace and Secretary of the Select Committee.

---

[1] The summons to Mr Bolts to appear before the Board on the charge of defrauding the Company with a bogus signature to his covenant is entered in the records of the Bengal Council of the 29th of August 1768, and the hearing was fixed for the 5th of September following.

The matter of the information ought also to be considered. It suggests merely an accusation for signing the new covenants not with his own hand but by his writer, which Mr Bolts will be advised by his Council was equally binding in law with his own signature, and they will excuse it by saying that no man of common sense could be absurd enough to think otherwise, that his inducement to it might be an idle but innocent one, to evade a rash oath which he had sworn that he would never sign them.

Baber's evidence indeed goes materially further than the information and charges him with a different offence, tho' not put in issue, viz., with endeavouring artfully to procure a re-delivery of the deed into his own custody, with some bad design not explained by the witness, and therefore it is impossible to say what the offence is, under colour of re-executing it.

Besides this, the summons is defective in not specially requiring Mr Bolts to shew cause why he should not be removed (according to the special authority given by the charter) from the office of Alderman on account of his offence, whereas neither the summons nor information takes any notice of his removal or what was intended by them, and the sentence pronounced against him of the 5th September 1768 only declares him disqualified, but is no formal or regular judgment of amotion or removal.

Some of these objections might probably be held too strict in an action for damages brought by Mr Bolts against the President and Council, but if the amotion should be deemed valid in a court of law in England, still it seems necessary to have given a new notice for his departure out of India after such removal from his office of Alderman, and that the time which intervened between the day of his sentence and the day of seizing his person, that is between the 5th and 23rd September, was by much too short.[1] On the other hand it is true that the President and Council appear to have acted without any ill intention towards the Company, but not with the coolness and circumspection we could have wished.

As to Mr Bolts's complaints that witnesses were not permitted to be examined in support of his petition or presentment to the Grand Jury on the 27th May 1768, there is no doubt but that the offer made by the Court to adjourn to another day in order that the witnesses might be regularly summoned or served with subpoenas was consistent with justice and the rules of proceeding. Neither the prosecutor nor the Grand Jury were entitled to the aid of the Court upon the sudden for the purpose of compelling witnesses in the manner it was attempted. But if the witnesses had been duly served

---

[1] The fear that Mr Bolts would evade seizure and deportation, by means of a collusive judgment and arrest for debt, was very probably the reason for the final precipitance of the Council's action.

with subpoenas to appear, in that case any objections to the examination of them arising from the duty of their offices and obligations to secrecy must have been made by the witnesses themselves at the time of the examination and proposed to the Court for their judgment.

We are clearly of opinion upon the whole that the proceedings against Mr Bolts have not been sufficiently regular and cautious, and that the event of an action for false imprisonment (if any should be brought hereafter) against the President or any of the Council will depend much on the impression which the various circumstances of the case may make upon a jury. If Mr Bolts shall appear to the Court to have been well removed from his office as Alderman and to have acted with insolence towards his superiors and in breach of his duty to the Company, he will fail in his action. But in case his amotion from his corporate office shall be held illegal, it is probable that he will recover considerable damages as a person seized and sent home without warrant from the statute, and consequently contrary to law.

It is indeed matter of astonishment to us that Mr Bolts who was under a sentence of suspension in August 1766 should during that period be elevated into the office of Alderman by the President and Council, who only could chuse him, which office tho' it confess in him no authority or license to trade after actual resignation or dismission, yet certainly it impowers him to reside in India and obliges him to perform the duty of his office for life, unless he should be guilty of some offence amounting to a just cause of dismission or amotion from that office according to the Charter of Justice.

The Select Committee most clearly was not impowered to act in a judicial capacity. They can administer no oath nor compell persons or partys to appear before them either to give evidence or to answer accusations or charges against them, nor can they make decree or pronounce legal judgments. In matters very important and interesting to the Company they do well to enquire into and investigate them to the bottom, but this must be done upon voluntary information and evidence. The partys accused should have reasonable notice and time given to justify themselves if they can. Whether they chuse to appear or not, if upon good evidence, which when taken *vivâ voce* the witnesses must be sworn before a magistrate capable of administering an oath who should likewise be present at the examination and discussion of the matter, or if taken in writing, such depositions made out and supported. In case the matter should be an object of civil jurisdiction, there is a court of justice legally established before which such offences should be brought and tried. If the charges so proved should not be proper subjects of civil or criminal jurisdiction, but rather of a political nature tending to affect the Company's rights and interests or to disturb the government and repose of the country, we think that although the Select Committee may have power to dismiss from the Company's service, suspend, or censure the guilty party, yet it would be more prudent to let such dismissions, suspensions, or censures proceed from the President and Council in their public capacity and as their act. There may be times and circumstances when this may be impolitick or improper, and therefore what is now suggested is more properly matter of advice and recommendation than absolute direction, as we are sensible no general rule or order can be established.

The creditors of Mr William Bolts have presented a request to us agreeable to the enclosed copy desiring we would send directions to our several settlements to give every necessary and proper assistance to his attornies or agents for collecting and remitting to England his outstanding concerns. It is therefore our positive direction that you comply with their request accordingly."

CHAPTER XVII

MR BOLTS'S ATTORNEYS AND THE BENGAL COUNCIL

WHEN Mr Bolts was removed from Bengal, he left the settlement of his affairs in the hands of a firm of Calcutta solicitors, who very soon found themselves involved in a wordy warfare with the Council. The correspondence that ensued is somewhat tedious and not particularly interesting, except as showing the reluctance of the Council to carry out the Company's express orders to facilitate the recovery of Mr Bolts's outstanding concerns. The correspondence commences with the reply of his solicitors dated the 13th of October 1769 to the demand for payment of the amount decreed against him on the Benares grain contract. They refer the Company's solicitor to Mr Bolts in England, who has left them no instructions on this point.

On the 8th of January 1770 they claim to set off Mr Bolts's legal expenses incurred in the litigation over the grain contract, amounting to Rs. 1873/1/3, together with the balance due to the Company, Rs. 130/6/6, against the amount tendered by Mr Bolts on account of salt balances and rice ("which was then refused and a suit commenced in the Mayor's Court for a larger sum,") viz. Rs. 3175/7/9.

The President and Council having demanded a formal attestation of the correctness of Mr Bolts's statement of his outstanding concerns, Messrs Reed and Cator, his solicitors, forward on the 12th of January the required attestation, and propose to pursue the same method in future applications for assistance from the Council.   They also send a general conspectus of Mr Bolts's commercial affairs, which shows the extent and complexity of his business transactions :

"(a) in Sylhet—copper and outstanding balances, value Rs. 5000 and upwards.   Some merchants, who had contracted to supply 'muggadooties'[1] in exchange for copper, are trying to repudiate their bargain and return the copper.   They want an order on the Faujdar of Sylhet to see justice done in the affair.

(b) At Dacca—goods and debts valued at Rs. 32/500.   There is an Armenian gomastah there named Coja Miguel Sarkis[2] for the provision of cloths, etc., on account of Mr Bolts.   By his last account there were balances due to the amount of Rs. 24,000, together with goods in hand to the value of Rs. 1000 in gold thread and Rs. 7500 in copper purchased at the Company's sales.   They want an order to the Chief and Council at Dacca for the recovery of the amount and dustucks for the transmission of the dutiable commodities.

(c) At Khulnea—due from various Zemindars Rs. 127,000.   They want perwannahs on these Zemindars, ordering them either to pay up the balances due immediately, or, if that is out of their power, to give fresh contracts for salt to Mr William Bolts on the same terms as to other merchants who pay ready money.

(d) At Conjere or Khanjah.   Here there are 34,000 maunds of salt belonging to Mr Bolts and balances due to the amount of Rs. 12,900.   They make the same request as above for permission to substitute the renewal of salt contracts for ready money payment, and for dustucks.

(e) At Banssen Ghautta—6000 maunds of salt.

(f) At Tomlook—Here 2000 maunds of salt have been detained and Rs. 230 extorted in irregular fees by the native officials.   They request an order for restitution, with interest and damages.

(g) At Salkee—1000 maunds of salt.

(h) At Patna—3000 maunds of betel-nut, which arrived soon after the Committee for salt, beetlenut, and tobacco was dissolved as per advertisement, but was by order of Mr Thomas Rumbold

---

[1] Silk dhotis.   Lieut.-Col. P. R. T. Gurdon, the Assamese scholar and ethnologist, has suggested that 'mugga' represents the Assamese 'mūga,' silk-worm, in spite of the objection that 'mūga' should have been transliterated into 'mooga,' not 'mugga.'   His opinion is confirmed by Dr J. D. Anderson, Cambridge University Reader in Bengali, and by Professor Sunith Kumar Chatterji.   Silk garments are considered as ceremonially pure, and are worn in religious worship.   I am greatly indebted to Col. Gurdon and to Dr Anderson for the trouble which they have both taken to elucidate the word.

[2] See page 66.

forbid being brought on shore; however by paying of bribes to sundry people to the amount of about Rs. 700 it was landed, but not permitted to be sold, though many purchasers would have been glad to buy it at 12 rupees a maund. . . . The damages Mr Bolts sustained by these measures were Rs. 7200 (through loss on sale, and bribes). 'We request the favour of your information to whom we are to apply for the said sums of money.'

(*i*) Salt duties—They want a refund of salt duties paid on 8300 maunds; the particulars will follow; the purchasers have deducted the amount 'since the putting up of the advertisements at the Court House respecting the collection of imports or dutys on salt to be paid.' To whom are they to apply for a refund? They press for an early answer."

To these two communications the Board replied as follows on the 16th of January :

"The Company have informed them of Mr Bolts's readiness to pay the balance due to them, viz. Rs. 3175/7/9, and directed them to receive this sum, but make no mention of any deductions, and are ignorant of any lawsuits having been carried on.[1] The Board therefore refuse to admit any deductions and demand payment in full. A Perwannah will be granted on the Faujdar of 'Sallet,'[2] and a letter sent to the Chief and Council of Dacca.

As the Board 'have every reason to imagine that the rest of the demands which Mr Bolts hath made, and which are specified in your letter are on account of contracts made for salt, which is a direct and manifest breach of the Company's express orders publicly issued by advertisement, they can never imagine the Company meant, when they gave directions to afford you effectual assistance in collecting in Mr Bolts's outstanding concerns, that the Board should assist you in collecting unlawful concerns; or that the Company could conceive Mr Bolts's demands were of such a nature.' Nor do the Board think it is in their power to afford Mr Bolts any assistance in the recovery of the balances incurred by an illicit trade publicly prohibited by the Company. 'On reference to the Custom House it nowhere appears that Mr Bolts hath paid any duties on salt; the Board cannot therefore conceive what title he hath to any demands on that account.'"

The orders of the Court of Directors, referred to in

[1] An extraordinary misstatement. In their letter of the 17th of March 1769, which must have been received long before this date, the Directors pronounced judgment on the Council's litigation with Mr Bolts respecting the Benares grain contract. See page 45.
[2] Sylhet.

the preceding correspondence, were those issued on Mr Bolts's petition in their letter of the 30th of June 1769 :

" Mr William Bolts who returned hither from your Presidency on the *Valentine* having represented that by your obliging him to leave Bengal, his own and the fortunes of several for whom he was concerned to the amount of upwards of £110,000 are left at the mercy of the natives in different parts of the country, and that the greatest part thereof under the oppressions he has suffered, he apprehends will never be received without our interposition. We therefore direct that you give Mr Bolts's attornies, Messrs Keir, Reed, Cator, and Gibson, effectual assistance upon all such applications as they may find necessary to make to you for facilitating the recovery of his outstanding concerns, as well as those of his constituents in the different parts of the country, and you have herewith a copy of his application to us on this subject for your government."

The orders which the President and Council had received from the Directors were, therefore, sufficiently explicit and peremptory to cover *all* applications for assistance which Mr Bolts's representatives thought it necessary to make, and the refusal of the Bengal Council to include salt, one of the most important commodities in Mr Bolts's business transactions, was certainly not justified by the terms of the instructions they had received. It is difficult to avoid the suspicion that the private interests of the members of Council had not a little to do with their disobedience to the plain directions of their superiors on this point, especially as we know that salt was a favourite article of commerce with members of Council; both Governor Verelst and Colonel Smith had had extensive dealings in that article, and Mr Barwell, who was now a member of the Board, afterwards, made the greater part of his ample fortune by his salt contracts.

On the 22nd of January Messrs Reed and Cator replied with a refusal to pay any more on the grain contract than the balance due after deducting Mr Bolts's legal expenses, and expressed surprise at the Secretary's statement in his letter of the 16th instant, that the Board " are ignorant of any lawsuits having been carried on." They convey their thanks for the promise of a perwannah to the Faujdar of Sylhet, and for the letter written to the Chief and Council of Dacca. They are surprised at the objection raised to the salt contracts in the Secretary's last letter as in his previous letter of the 11th instant he raised none, but on the contrary assured them of the Board's assistance in recovering Mr Bolts's dues; the objection is the more annoying, as they had given Mr Bolts's creditors hope of speedy payment. They contend that all these salt contracts were *concluded* before the issue of the Board's orders mentioned by the Secretary, and observe :

"Mr Bolts apprehends such orders or advertisements could not affect his transactions being antecedent, and those others relative to future ones. We cannot presume,"

they continue,

"to judge what the Company meant by their directions further than by the tenor of them. In Mr Bolts's letter to the Court of Directors dated London the 26th May 1769 he mentions (with other places) his concerns at Roymungul, Kulnea, Ingellee, and Hougly, and as there are now gentlemen in the Direction who have a competent knowledge of the trade of Bengal, and what returns are to be had from the different places specified in his said letter, they consequently knew that from those above-mentioned places he could have no outstanding balances to collect in or goods to export excepting salt or for salt, as it is notorious that excepting very trifling ones there are no other articles of commerce in those places, and by his said letter it seems natural to conclude that his concerns there were capital; we therefore with all due deference think the Court of Directors would particularly have excepted to that article, had not their intention been as general as their order, of which Mr Bolts has procured and sent us a copy."

They remark that the settlement of Mr Bolts's affairs, debtor and creditor, depends chiefly on the salt. All the salt contracts (with one trivial exception), were made by and on account of John Matthias Ross, Esq., from whom also Mr Bolts bought them at a premium, and consequently they are prior both to the Board's orders and advertisements and to the Nabob's perwannah. They enumerate the sums paid as salt duty. An exact account of Mr Bolts's loss thereby will be furnished, if required. They request a letter to " Nabob Sujah al Dowlah," to obtain the performance of nine perwannahs granted to Mr Bolts on his Zemindars for 27,000 rupees' worth of saltpetre, a copy of the letter, and an early answer. They will be "under the disagreeable necessity" of sending home protests to Mr Bolts, in case of any refusals.

Nevertheless they give an assurance that they desire to do their duty to Mr Bolts without discourtesy to the Board, and hope their zeal for their client will not involve the Board's disapprobation of their conduct. They conclude with a decidedly improper and offensive reference to the late President,

"Mr Verelst having many times declared himself our enemy, as also to the partnership we were lately connected with, merely for acting with that fidelity to Mr Bolts which we presume ought to have been our recommendation, we hope will apologise for this intrusion, not that we apprehend there is any reason to expect such prepossessions against us from the gentlemen now presiding at your Board."

To this letter the Board replied on the following day :

" The Board will receive the amount tendered, Rs. 1301/6/6, only as part payment of the demand made ; if they refuse to pay it on this understanding, the matter must be referred to the Directors. They propound a dilemma for Mr Bolts, that he violated either his agreement with the Society of Trade, or the Company's orders. ' If the contracts for salt entered into by Mr Bolts were made, or if he bought them of any person, before the Society of Trade was dissolved, his claim is invalidated by the agreement he entered into with that Society, and he is liable to the penalty stipulated.

If, on the other hand, it was a transaction after the Society was dissolved, he was then guilty of a breach of the Company's orders and acted in direct opposition to the restrictive perwannah issued by the Nabob.' So that, in either case, Mr Bolts cannot properly claim the Board's assistance, nor they grant it.

If the demands upon the Zemindars under the authority of the

Nabob Sujah al Dowlah were made in consequence of actual
advances received, the Board would readily make the application to
His Excellency you desire; but as it does not appear to them that
these perwannahs have been granted for advances made by Mr
Bolts, they rather conceived it to be an act of indulgence shown him
by His Excellency, in granting them before Mr Bolts had made
advances, which the Nabob may revoke at pleasure, and not a
mercantile transaction wherein Mr Bolts can claim their assistance.

I must now inform you, gentlemen, that the Board are greatly
surprised and displeased at the very unbecoming reflection you have
cast upon Mr Verelst, a reflection which they deem highly improper
in you to make, and equally injurious to the character of that
gentleman."

On receipt of this communication, Mr Bolts's representatives made a sworn protest before the Notary
Public, in which they declare that the Board have dis-
obeyed the orders of the Court of Directors, by refusing to aid them in collecting Mr Bolts's balances, and
consequently, as they cannot settle his affairs, they
hold the Board[1] responsible for all losses. On the
27th of January they sent a copy of this protest to the
Board, accompanied by the following letter :

They refuse to pay the Rs. 130/6/6 except in return for a receipt
in full. As to the salt contracts, they advance the extraordinary
argument that a man is not bound by an existing contract, if he
knows that it is soon about to terminate.

" As the contracts for salt were made after it was publicly known
that the Society of Trade was to be dissolved by order of the Court
of Directors and prior to any restrictive perwannahs issued by the
Nabob, Mr Bolts deems his purchase legal either with respect to the
Society or the Company's orders; but having received your determinations on that head, we will not intrude further on your time
regarding it. We request the favour of your answer concerning the
loss sustained by Mr Bolts on his beetlenut at Patna, as mentioned
in our letter to you of the 8th instant, and also your resolution with
respect to the letter to the Nabob Sujah al Dowlah we apply'd to
you for in our last, as the paragraph in your Secretary's letter of the
23rd instant seems to be rather an opinion than your determination
on that subject.

We are sorry, gentlemen, that you have taken offence at the

---

[1] The following gentlemen were on the Board at this date, Messrs
Cartier, Russell, Floyer, Hare, Jekyll, and Barwell.

H

mention made of Mr Verelst in our last, for tho' true in all its circumstances, had we thought it would have displeased you, we would have been silent on the subject."

To this letter the Board vouchsafed no reply, and the correspondence dropped for a time. It was re-opened in the following November by a letter from Messrs Reed and Cator, in which they repeated their previous requests for the Board's assistance in collecting Mr Bolts's balances, alluded to the Directors' repetition of their previous orders in their letter of the 23rd March 1770,[1] and enclosed a second formal protest against the Board's refusal to obey those orders.

The Board's answer was to the effect that they had already assisted them as far as possible by letters sent to Sylhet and Dacca. They refused to give any assistance regarding salt and betel-nut contracts " their duty to the Company not permitting them to assist any person in the recovery of balances incurred in an illicit trade prohibited by the Company." They repeated their reply of the 23rd of January with respect to the nine perwannahs granted by " Nabob Sujah al Dowlah."

With this last letter the correspondence ended.

[1] See above, page 106. The Directors again repeated these orders, on an application from Mr Bolts's creditors, in their despatch of the 7th of April 1773. In the Court minutes for February 1770 Messrs Thomas Hay and Ralph Leycester appear as Mr Bolts's foremost creditors on this occasion.

CHAPTER XVIII

MR BOLTS IN ENGLAND

AFTER his return to England Mr Bolts devoted all the energies of his vigorous, if uncultivated, intelligence to the task of revenging himself upon his enemies of the Bengal administration and of injuring the reputation and prosperity of the East India Company. Considering that he fought the battle practically singlehanded against all the wealth and political influence of that great corporation, it is a remarkable tribute to his ability and pertinacity that he should have succeeded in ruining ex-Governor Verelst by litigation, in stirring up a strong feeling in England against the Company, and in inflicting a serious blow upon their commerce in the East Indies.[1]

His first success was scored in his appeal to the Privy Council against the judgment of the Mayor's Court, confirmed on appeal in Calcutta, removing him from his seat as Alderman of the Mayor's Court.

Writing in March 1770, the Directors censure the Council for their omission to send the proceedings in this case properly authenticated:

"By the *Shrewsbury* we received your answer to Mr Bolts's appeal to the King and Council for removing him from being an Alderman of the Mayor's Court, but you have omitted to send the proceedings relating thereto properly authenticated under the seal

---

[1] Considering his attitude to the Company, it is somewhat surprising to find him coolly applying to them in February 1770 for a loan to tide him over his pecuniary difficulties until he receives his remittances from Bengal. The Directors refused this modest request.

of the Company, so as to become evidence before the Lords of the Council, which you ought certainly to have done, and more especially as they were granted to Mr Bolts or his attorney, as set forth in his petition to his Majesty, to which we have been obliged to have recourse. You must not fail sending by the first opportunity in duplicate all the proceedings respecting his removal under the seal of the Company, and attested by the Clerk of appeals, and in all cases for the future when you have any apprehension that appeals are intended, you must forthwith send the proceedings properly authenticated under the seal of the Company to be made use of here for their defence. You will observe that your answer to Mr Bolts's petition of appeal lodged in India constitutes no part of the proceedings, for it was out of course and practice to make any answer to either by way of plea, demurrer, or otherwise; nor is any part of the proceedings in the Mayor's Court relevant to this sentence against Mr Bolts, which could only be brought before the Governor and Council. Therefore the transcript and copy you are to transmit is to end with your letter giving notice of your judgment and his removal from the office of Alderman to the Mayor's Court."

Long before this letter was received, judgment was given in favour of Mr Bolts. In their letter of the 27th of June 1770, the Directors announce the result, and issue instructions with regard to the further suits pending against the Company's servants in Bengal:

"His Majesty having approved of the report of the Lords of his Privy Council and their sentence therein mentioned, whereby the judgment given by you for removing Mr William Bolts from the office of one of the Aldermen of the Mayor's Court of Calcutta is reversed, and he is restored to his said office pursuant to his appeal to his Majesty.—And we having in consequence of the said sentence of reversal signified to him our expectation that he repair to Calcutta in one of the Company's ships of the ensuing season in order to resume the functions of the said office, you must acquaint Mr Lawrell who was appointed to fill up Mr Bolts's vacancy as an Alderman that he must relinquish that office and is no longer to act in that capacity after his receipt of your notice."

On receipt of a copy of this extract enclosed in a letter dated the 14th of March 1771, the Registrar of the Mayor's Court writes to the Board on the 2nd of April to acknowledge its receipt and to inform them that

"Mr William Bolts is again restored to his former seat of Alderman of this Court, conformable to the sentence pronounced by his Majesty in Council. I am further to inform you that Mr Robert Crawford, one of the Aldermen of the said Court having obtained leave of the Court to resign his seat as an Alderman of the said Court, thereby the number of Aldermen of the said Court became compleat conformable to his late most Gracious Majesty's charter."

Mr Bolts, however, had won only a Pyrrhic victory. The Company's invitation to him to embark on one of their vessels of the next season was coupled with the intimation that permission to reside in Bengal did not carry with it any licence to trade. The salary attached to the office was no inducement to a man of Mr Bolts's position, and the only value which he attached to the right of residence in Bengal consisted in the opportunity for prosecuting his private trade. Besides, he was absorbed in his legal and literary attacks on the Company, and could not immediately avail himself of the offer.[1] Consequently the right accorded to him by the judgment of the Privy Council lapsed through his failure to take his seat as Alderman, though he made an attempt in May 1771 to retain his right by applying for a passage on the *Britannia*, via Bombay,[2] and in August 1771 the Directors inform the President and Council that they have received

[1] In July 1770, however, he applied to the Directors for permission to remain in England two years before proceeding "to his station in the Mayor's Court of Calcutta."

[2] In a despatch of the 12th of June 1771, the Directors announced Mr Bolts's impending return to India: "Mr William Bolts having applied to us for permission to take passage to Bombay on the *Britannia* in order to proceed to Bengal to resume the office of an Alderman in the Mayor's Court at Calcutta. We have thought proper to comply with his request, and have positively directed that he be not permitted to stay longer at Bombay than until the first conveyance that may offer either by an Europe or Country ships sailing for your Presidency on which he is to embark."

the opinions of the most eminent counsel in the kingdom to the effect that

"the office of Alderman of the Mayor's Court, to which Mr Bolts was ordered to be restored upon an appeal to his Majesty in Council, is, according to the Charter of Justice become vacant. The Board is, therefore, ordered to proceed to choose a successor according to the said charter."

In their letter of June 1770, the Directors issued the following instructions in view of the other suit then pending :

" As Mr Bolts hath instituted a suit at law against the Company's servants, it is absolutely necessary for their defence that you send the following particulars, first taking three copies thereof duly attested to be disposed of as hereafter mentioned, viz. Mr Bolts's original letters to the Governor and Council and Select Committee from 1764 to his departure from Bengal, his original protests, petitions, and remonstrances, his original letters to Messrs Beecher and Alexander, if they can be procured, also those to Mr Droz,[1] or any of the Company's servants, Brigadier-General Smith's original letters concerning Mr Bolts, the original intercepted letter from Mr Bolts to Mr Gentil, his original information and petition to the jurors on the 27th May 1768, and Mahomed Reza Cawn's letter mentioned in consultations 15th August 1768, and any other original papers that have passed relative to Mr Bolts."

Elaborate instructions are also given by which the commander and chief and second mates of each vessel entrusted with the conveyance of either of the duplicate sets of copies of these documents

"shall examine the copies with the originals, that they may be able to give evidence thereon ; the Company's seal is to be affixed to all documents sent by the Board, and the seal of the Mayor's Court to documents sent thence ; a duly attested authentic copy of the whole correspondence is to be kept amongst the Board's records."

In 1769 was published Mr Bolts's first attempt to appeal to a wider public than that of Bengal against his oppressors. It is a curious little tract, published

[1] Simeon Droz, Secretary to the Board.

in London in that year, entitled "Extracts from the Public Advertiser relative to the oppressions suffered in Bengal by Mr William Bolts and his Armenian Agents from the East-India Company's Representatives there." Besides his petition to the Directors, quoted above, it contains detailed references to the affairs of Nobkissen and Ramnant, an account of the fate of his petition, a denial of the accusation of intriguing with Shuja-u-Daula and others, attacks upon the Select Committee, a summary of the reforms required in Bengal, and a copy of the petition of the three Armenian merchants to the Directors. It is prefaced by an address to the Proprietors of East India Stock:[1]

"Gentlemen,—Conceiving myself injured in the most inhuman manner, and that the liberty and property of every British subject residing in Bengal is involved in my case, and in consequence the capital stock of every Proprietor of the East India Company is deeply affected in the decision, since there can be no security in any Government in the absence of justice, I presume to lay a short abstract of my particular hardships before the public, hoping that this nation, which has been so celebrated for its humanity, and so remarkable in attending to the sufferings of individuals, when affecting the great principles of the Constitution, will not be inattentive to my case: however low I must place myself as an individual in the community.

In this Address to the Public, I am far from meaning the least disrespect to the Honourable Court of Directors; on the contrary it has been my intention to follow that method of seeking redress, which could be conceived the most respectful to them. I had observed since the tyrannies began to multiply in Bengal, that of the many persons who had been injured beyond example in the history of our Government, not one had obtained any redress, or that any punishment or censure had been inflicted on the perpetrators of the most horrid crimes.

Upon arriving in England, buoyed up with those notions which

---

[1] From the Minutes of a General Court held on the 30th October 1771 it appears that Mr Bolts was at that date himself a Proprietor, as his name is entered as one of those who vote for a motion that Mr Bolts should be furnished with the minutes, answers, or remarks of the Governor and Council of Calcutta on his memorial of the 5th September 1768.

it is natural for a man to entertain, who had learnt more from books than practice concerning the liberty and protection which a subject may now expect from the British Government, I eagerly enquired into the cause of this seeming paradox. Some informed me that the Company's affairs had been governed for several years past by an illiberal and desperate faction, stranger to every principle of a just Government, and whose only rule of right had been to support their friends at all events, and to depress those whom they deemed their enemies by every means, legal or illegal, without enquiring farther into any complaint. Others informed me, that the whole of this irregularity had proceeded from Gentlemen claiming redress from tumultuous General Courts, without making proper applications to the Court of Directors : to whom in the opinion of the most discreet members of the Company the consideration of such points did properly belong. Accordingly, in pursuance of the last mentioned advice, and agreeably to my own sentiments, which point out every kind of deference to men in authority which does not supersede that equal and manly spirit with which an ingenuous mind is always prepared to resist oppression, I presented to the Honourable Court of Directors, on the 19th of May, the following Petition . . ."

The general indictment which Mr Bolts laid before the Proprietors against the Government of Bengal was as follows :

"As the regulations necessary for the well-conducting of your affairs in Bengal have lately become matter of debate at your General Courts, and are universally the subjects of conversation, I hope the following assertions from one just arrived, and not unacquainted with the interior police[1] of that country, will not be deemed unworthy of your serious consideration :

With respect to justice,

1st. That there are not the necessary checks to secure the due administrations of justice in the Settlement of Calcutta, or in any other part of your dominions under that Presidency.

2ndly. That particularly in Calcutta the Governor and Counsellors being the only magistrates, Judges at the Sessions, and Justices of the Peace, whenever they choose it, they can and do with great convenience transfer any complainant from the Counsellor to the Justice of the Peace, from the Justice of the Peace to the Zemindar, from the Zemindar to the Secret Committee, and from the Secret Committee to the Nabob, with whom they can do what they please, and vice versâ.

---

[1] Perhaps a clerical error for "policy."

3rdly. That if a complaint be brought before them at the General Quarter Sessions, and the Governor and Council (tho' then in their capacity of Judges) do not choose it should be heard, they can and have put a stop to such proceedings, whereby the plaintiff is left without remedy in the Settlement.

4thly. That the Mayor and Aldermen of the Mayor's Court, who take cognizance only of affairs of meum and tuum, are also appointed by the Governor and Council, who pretend to a right of dismissing, and do actually dismiss them upon the most frivolous pretexts, without confronting the party with his accuser, or allowing him time to appeal according to the directions of the charter.

5thly. That in short the Governor and Council of Calcutta having the legislative, judicial, and executive powers in their own hands, together with the beforesaid means of evasion, are above the reach of justice in that Settlement; while the natives (who are a polite, civilized, and mild people) when labouring under tyranny and oppression, have no redress but by coming to England, by which from their religious tenets they would be exposed to expulsion from their casts or tribes, an ignominy which they esteem worse than death.

With respect to trade, I assert,

6thly. That the Regulations in force in Bengal are highly oppressive and injurious to the manufacturers: particularly one, whereby no person is allowed to purchase any goods in the Inland country without an order of permission called a perwanah under the hand and seal of the Governor of Calcutta.

7thly. That the above and other oppressive regulations, too numerous to be here mentioned, have gradually decreased the number of manufacturers, debased the manufactures, and enabled those in power to establish ruinous monopolies.

8thly. That a most striking and recent instance of such monopolies, not to be paralleled in the history of any Government, is the Governor and Council engrossing the cotton, imported by sea from Surat, employing the Nabob and his officers to sell it for them at their own prices, and through the Nabob preventing the inland importation of that staple, in order to enhance their own sales.

9thly. That many thousands of merchants, who used to come down into our provinces from the north and westward with ready money to purchase the manufactures of Bengal, discouraged by these obstructions and difficulties, with their consequences, have now totally left off that tract; whereby we have long been deprived of that valuable trade, which alone would be sufficient to supply the country with bullion almost equal to our exportation to China, and other demands, and

10thly. In support of the above it will be found upon examination that there is not a weaver or manufacturer throughout the country (those under the protection of the foreign Companies excepted) but who is *forced* to furnish the gomastahs or agents of the Company and their representatives with their goods at prices from 15 to 50 per cent. less than those very manufacturers could get from their next door neighbours, if left at liberty to sell to whom they pleased.   Such, Gentlemen, is the present state of Bengal, and the situation of our countrymen there, but particularly of the black inhabitants, to whose industry we are and must continue to be indebted for the advantages we expect to reap from those territories. I have spoken of some of those grievances because I have laboured under them and feel them, and because I have suffered for daring to shew I felt them.   It is not, however, a private but a national cause which engages me to speak on this head ; for I am of opinion that there is no one foreign concern (America excepted) which is at this period more deserving of the attention of the British Nation than the due Regulation and Government of our possessions in the East Indies. I have therefore presumed to submit to your consideration the above crude hints, before you determine upon Regulations which must be of the greatest importance.   Nothing less than the prosperity or the ruin, the preservation or the loss of the country depend upon those Regulations.   If the present grievances be not redressed, and proper Laws and Regulations made, you will at some future period run a greater risque from the Natives themselves than from all your foreign enemies together.   If equitable Regulations and salutary Laws be made and carried into execution, you will then engage the hearts and minds of those natives who wish only to receive their protection and happiness from you : In such a situation you might brave the combined efforts of your Indian enemies, tho' they were assisted by all our European rivals."

A copy of the petition presented to the Directors by " Gregore Cojamaul and Johannes Padre Rafael, Armenian merchants, late of Bengal " is next introduced as follows :

"Besides the above named Armenian Gentlemen there were also two others named Cogee Melcomb Philip and Cogee Wuscan Stephen, who were at the same time confined and treated in the same manner as above related :   And to so great a pitch did the Governor and Council carry the inveteracy of their private pique against Mr Bolts, that the Armenian merchants were thus ill-treated solely because in the course of their mercantile business they had also, as agents, transacted some business for him : they having never been accused of any misbehaviour, nor was there ever any other reason for this ill-treatment than Mr Verelst's minute upon the Consultations as contained in the Petition to the Court of Directors of the 19th May 1769, page 10. The other Armenian merchant, Wuscan Stephen, had like many others been established many years in business in that country and never acted as agent for Mr Bolts, or any other English gentleman, but being very frequently in company with the other Armenians he was suspected of being Mr Bolts's agent and imprisoned as such to the great loss and almost total ruin of himself and his family; though he never had had any connections with Mr Bolts: The intention (among other purposes to be served) was to injure Mr Bolts in his private fortune, and there cannot be a more striking instance of the inveterate oppression with which Mr Bolts was persecuted."

In 1772 Mr Bolts fulfilled his threat of adding to the national odium against the Company by the publication of his book entitled "Considerations on India affairs, particularly respecting the present state of Bengal and its dependencies. By William Bolts, 1772, Merchant and Alderman, or Judge of the Mayor's Court of Calcutta." The book stirred up so much popular interest in the affairs of the Company, and so greatly prejudiced the public mind against the Company and its servants in Bengal, that ex-Governor Verelst was invited by the Directors to reply to Mr Bolts's charges. It was also translated into French by J. N. Demeunnier[1] in 1775 and published in Paris under the title "Etat civil, etc., du Bengale," and again reproduced in French in 1838 as "Histoire des Conquêtes et de l'administration de la Compagnie Anglaise au Bengale. Par William Bolts, ancien membre du conseil des revenus à Benares et alderman de la cour du maire à Calcutta."

An attack upon the "Nabobs," published in the following year, and entitled "The Nabob, or Asiatic Plunderers. A satyrical Poem," contains an allusion to Mr Bolts's work:

"Again, Sir, I aver what first I said;
Conscience in some, and moral sense is dead.

---

[1] Afterwards a member of the States-general.

> Could they from murder, rapine, famine too,
> Amassing wealth, if Dow and Bolts speak true?
> Could they, if conscience were not quite asleep,
> Each day, a Saturnalian revel keep?"

Alexander Dow was the author of "The History of Hindostan, translated from the Persian," published 1770.

Mr Bolts's book was also mentioned by Lord Clive in his speech before the House of Commons.

The counterblast, a quarto volume, appeared later in the same year, 1772. It was entitled "A view of the rise, progress, and present state of the English Government in Bengal, including a reply to the misrepresentations of Mr Bolts and other writers."

By Harry Verelst, Esq., Late Governor of Bengal.

Difficilius est provincias obtinere, quam facere :
Viribus parantur, jure retinentur.

Flori Libr. iv. c. 12.

To this work Mr Bolts replied in 1775 with Volume II of his "Considerations," a still bulkier book than Volume I, enriched with no less than 632 pages of appendices. In the first chapter he insinuates that Verelst was editor rather than author of the work which had appeared in his name :

"Mr Henry Verelst, late Govenor of Bengal and principal defendant in the writer's suits, hath since caused a book to be published with his name prefixed to it, in which it evidently appears to have been his chief view to invalidate the strong charges and informations contained in "Considerations on India Affairs"; by heaping groundless accusations, with illiberal invectives on their author; for to that one purpose have Mr Verelst's writers actually appropriated the first forty-two pages of their work."

In the preface to his book he poses as the victim of arbitrary power and the intrepid defender of British liberties :

"The writer of these sheets, who was many years in the service of the Company in Bengal, and is an Alderman or Judge at the

Mayor's Court of Calcutta,[1] agreeably to the charter, writes not with a view of advantage to himself. He has felt the iron rod of oppression from the Company and their servants, in'many instances equally grievous with any that are herein laid before the public; but having appealed for justice to the laws of this country (though it must be some years before he can obtain it) he forbears at present to say more of himself or his cause than that he was marked out for vengeance in Bengal for his professional abilities, even small as they were, and his success in such mercantile undertakings as rather entitled him to the blessings of the natives, as they were usefully obstructive to mischievous monopolists, and of service to the Company, though offensive to their principal servants. During the whole period of his servitude, he never had violated a law of this kingdom, or been guilty of any bad practice; but had always been faithful and zealous in the service of the Company, whose Directors he defies to lay before their constituents so much as a single charge that can vindicate their proceedings against him, or any accusation, grounded on truth or reason, to convict him of a breach of duty in any moral capacity or connection, or that will stand the test of candid scrutiny by any one man of real honour and understanding. Nevertheless, by the oppressions under which, single and unsupported, he has patiently suffered, he has actually lost sixty out of ninety thousand pounds sterling[2] of a fortune acquired by many years' industry in lawful and laudable commerce.

Thus much the Writer has presumed he was in justice authorised to say of himself, in order to obviate calumny, which is often added to persecution, for the sake of justifying it. He is sensible that this publication will even endanger his getting possession of a great part of the remainder of his scattered fortune; nevertheless, moderate and contented with what will remain to him, let what may be the consequence, he has at this critical juncture preferred to every other temporising view the discharge of his conscience, from a real and sincere regard to the welfare and rights of mankind in general, and to the interests of this kingdom in particular; for tho' he has not the honour of being a natural-born subject of Great Britain, yet being from his infancy bred in it, and having always lived among the natives of this happy country, he is in heart an Englishman and wishes to be no other, so long as the oppressed can obtain, from the English laws, justice adequate to their injuries."

---

[1] This was no longer true at the date of publication, for he had forfeited his seat by neglecting to take up his duties as Alderman. See above, page 118.

[2] Yet his Dutch biographer, amongst other misrepresentations, asserts that he suffered seven years' imprisonment and a fine of £94,000 sterling (Van der Aa's " Biographisch Woordenboch der Nederlanden)."

The Directors, he adds, will scarcely tax him with ingratitude, after having treated him with extreme cruelty, or blame him for exposing their secrets, when national benefit is the object in view. He concludes with the threat of publishing another volume, exhibiting documents of a still more curious and interesting nature.

Among the instances of oppression and of illegal measures taken by the President and Council in Bengal, Mr Bolts had cited in one of the numerous appendices to his "Considerations" the case of Captain John Nevill Parker, one of the officers implicated in the mutiny of 1766. At the very moment of publication this gentleman was anxiously awaiting a favourable reply to his humble petition for promotion,[1] and was not unnaturally apprehensive of the consequences of having unwittingly enlisted in his behalf so compromising a friend as Mr Bolts. In an undated letter laid before the Council on the 1st of September 1772, he writes to say that he has seen in a late publication of Mr Bolts "a very imperfect state of his case" in regard to the part he bore in the resignation of 1766, and solemnly declares that not only is this publication without his approbation, but that he positively refused his consent to it when approached by Mr Bolts. He objects strongly to being made to appear a party to "an ill-grounded and factious opposition" to the Company, at the very time when he has received the most generous marks of their lenity and forgiveness of his past errors, and is actually a candidate for future favours. He considers that the performance itself is too contemptible to be of any real hurt to the Company or their interests, but he would be extremely sorry to have appeared to countenance such a mode of appeal to the public. Only the error

---

[1] In their letter of the 10th of April 1771, the Directors had notified that he was readmitted to their service, and appointed to be a Captain of Infantry.

of his inexperienced youth has been mentioned; the forgiveness and generosity of the Directors is suppressed. He apologises for intruding on their notice, and hopes they will lay his real sentiments before the Directors, should they think Mr Bolts's performance is likely to injure his prospects.

It is instructive to compare Mr Bolts's vignette of himself with the full-length portrait of him drawn by Mr Verelst in his "Bengal":

"Mr Bolts arrived in India in the year 1760, and we soon find him a principal figure amongst the groups of traders. The extent to which this gentleman engaged, and the moderation with which he conducted himself, will be best known from his fortune of ninety thousand pounds, gained within six years, together with the extreme eagerness with which he endeavoured, upon all occasions, to degrade the authority of the government, and prevent any effectual protection being given to the natives.

Among the private persons who usurped the office of their superiors, Mr Bolts was early distinguished, who wrote in his own name to the fouzdar of Purnea, threatening the Nabob's officers with the effect of the English power."

Mr Verelst observes "of course every merchant will take the same authority," and very justly adds:

"this entire levelling and equality will not be for the good of the Company's affairs.

To level all distinctions, to intimidate the Governor and Council, and by clamour to confine them within the strict letter of laws calculated for a very different state of society, has ever been the constant object of those, who, from motives of private interest, wished to abuse that influence which the name of Englishman was alone sufficient to confer.

Notwithstanding Mr Bolts was reprimanded by order of the Court of Directors in the general letter to Bengal received in July 1764; yet, in the year 1765, we find him exercising summary jurisdiction in his own cause, and confining a merchant for three days, whom at length he was compelled to release. He was soon after this suspended from his appointment at Benares, but the trade of a country, yet unexhausted, was too lucrative to be easily relinquished.

The November following, Mr Bolts resigned his station in the service, and was about this time[1] elected an Alderman and Judge

---

[1] A very inaccurate statement; it was three months previously, on the 11th of August 1766, that he was appointed.

of the Mayor's Court in Calcutta. Here therefore commences his furious zeal for reformation, and, in the beginning of the next year, he was actively engaged in the complaint against Nobekissen, which ended with little honour to the authors. The public concerns of Mr Bolts never intruded upon his private cares, and infinite arts were tried to prevent the dismission of his agents from the dominions of Sujah al Dowlah. The great distance from Calcutta gave to falsehood the weight of truth. Various rumours were therefore propagated, which Mr Bolts endeavoured to support by his correspondence At one time Mr Bolts was returning to Benares with extensive powers. At another time these people were taken into Mr Rumbold's service, and a letter was on the road from the Council, that none should be licensed as English agents but themselves. While such arts were employed to influence the mind of the Nabob of Oude, the war upon the coast [1] had drained the treasury of Bengal, and the most alarming accounts were industriously spread of the instability of the Company's affairs. Allured by the tempting occasion, Sujah al Dowla began to listen to the voice of ambition. Coja Rafael, for the sake of intelligence, was taken into his service, through the influence of Meer Mushallah (formerly physician to Meer Kossim, and, at this time, retained by the Nabob of Oude) who likewise corresponded with our patriot at Calcutta. When the storm blew off, the dread of our power revived. Sujah al Dowla, again regarding the English agents as a source of contention, applied to our commanding officer at Allahabad for their removal; and both parties being now equally sincere, it was effected.

That Mr Bolts was a party to these practices cannot be doubted, when the reader is informed of a confidential letter written by that gentleman to Monsieur Gentil, a Frenchman, high in Sujah al Dowlah's confidence. . . ."

Here an extract is given from the letter which has been already quoted above.

"Such was the conduct of Mr Bolts and his agents, which produced at length the removal of the latter from the territories of Oude; and after every other expedient had been tried to reclaim a man, who appeared determined to sacrifice all public duties to his own interested pursuits, and who had actually presented to the Grand Jury an information against the Governor, Council, and Commander-in-Chief, for endeavouring to restrain his pernicious practices, Mr Bolts himself was sent to England. Instead of punishing Coja Gregory and Johannes Padre Rafael as they deserved, such was the idle lenity of our Government, that they immediately received their

---

[1] The Carnatic; the reference is to the first war with Haidar Ali.

liberty, and every assistance was offered to collect their effects, an assistance probably unnecessary, as they chose to depart for Europe.

That the measures of our government were sufficiently vigorous and decisive upon this, as upon other occasions, it might be difficult to prove;[1] but when Mr Bolts had been indulged with near two years, after his resignation of the service, to collect his effects; when the public authority had been employed, and letters written by the Governor to Bulwant Singh and the Nabob of Oude, requesting their assistance for the settlement of his affairs; it was surely no very ruinous oppression to send away that gentleman by force, whom the most solemn promises, repeatedly given, could not engage voluntarily to depart for Europe. The Governor and Council were indeed criminal. It was criminal for a moment to suffer the residence of a man,[2] who, independent of other demerits, had corresponded with every rival, and every enemy of the country, who had engaged with Mr Vernet, the Dutch Governor, to monopolize the cloth trade of Dacca; who had scandalously evaded the execution of covenants, which as a servant of the Company he was bound to subscribe; who had attempted one, and actually succeeded in seducing another, inferior servant, to betray his trust, in delivering papers out of the office; who had, from his first arrival in India, carried on a trade destructive to the peace of the country; who, in

---

[1] The weakness of the Bengal Government was due solely to the weakness of the Governor's character, as he himself appears dimly to have suspected. In his speech before the House of Commons in 1772 Lord Clive, an excellent judge of men, sketches the character of Mr Verelst, mentions the misgivings which he entertained on handing over the government of Bengal to him, and quotes his Farewell letter to the Select Committee in which he impressed on them the necessity of vigour in their measures and warned them of the danger of a relaxation of authority: "You have power, you have abilities, you have integrity:— let it not be said that you are deficient in resolution. I repeat, that you must not fail to exact the most implicit obedience to your orders . . . if you do not make a proper use of that power, with which you are invested, I shall hold myself acquitted, as I do now protest against the consequences."

Of Mr Verelst he said: "Mr Verelst . . . I do believe to be a man of as much real worth and honor as ever existed: and so far from being wanting in humanity, as Mr Bolts asserts, I know that he had too much humanity. Humanity, if I may be allowed the expression, has been his ruin. If he had had less, it would have been better for the nation, better for the Company, better for the natives, and better for himself. . . . He acted upon principles of disinterestedness from beginning to end. . . . But the truth is, he governed with too lenient a hand. The too great tenderness of his disposition, I saw and dreaded."

[2] It would have been interesting to hear Mr Verelst's defence of Mr Bolts's appointment to the office of Alderman.

I

support of this trade, had threatened the officers of the Nabob, and had issued his proclamation in the style of a sovereign ; whose agents by their intrigues in the dominions of Sujah al Dowlah, and by false intelligence received from their master, had endangered the peace of India. To suffer such a man in Bengal, was surely criminal. But if suits are now commenced in our courts of law, if petitions are presented to the House of Commons, and unwarrantable prejudices are industriously fomented, what might we expect, had ample justice been done to the Company and to the nation ? "

"Enough has been said to shew that the evils complained of in Bengal have arisen rather from the inability of the Governor and Council to restrain the daring and pernicious projects of private interest in others, than from a rapacious spirit in themselves. Had the higher servants of the Company, as the author of ' Considerations' would wish us to believe, been alone the oppressors of Bengal, the evil could not have extended far. But when the rapacity of all who assume the English name is let loose upon a harmless and inoffensive race of men ; when every attempt of the Governor and Council to restrain the lawless traders is represented as a violation of property and infringement of those laws by which only Europeans can be governed ; and when this spirit, supported by interested men, proceeds so far that the Governor and Council and Commander-in-chief are presented to the grand jury as conspirators against the life and fortune of an individual, we must not be surprized if gentlemen relax somewhat in the exercise of new, unknown, and questionable powers, however necessary to the welfare and safety of the province."

Whether Mr Verelst was the sole author of the work issued in his name, or was indebted to the literary assistance of others, as Mr Bolts insinuates, there can be no doubt that it contrasts favourably in style and in the moderation of its statements with the rather cheap rhetoric of Mr Bolts. It is interesting, moreover, from the direct, or implied, admissions which it makes, especially with regard to the strict legality of the measures taken against Mr Bolts.

In several of the suits instituted by the latter, in which Mr Verelst was defendant, or one of the defendants, he was cast in heavy damages in the years 1774 and 1775, and his fortune, originally ample, was so much impaired thereby that he was obliged to retire to the Continent, where he died, broken in health and spirits, in 1785.

Mr Bolts himself, who had only succeeded in realising about a third of his original fortune of £90,000, spent so much money in his litigation with the Company and its servants, and over the publication of his two volumes of "Considerations," that in the autumn of the year 1773 he became bankrupt,[1] and in the following year he was compelled to seek some means of repairing the sinews of war against the Company.

His first idea was to attack the interests of the Company in India through the Portuguese. But certain overtures that he made with that object to the Court of Lisbon, through the assistance of supporters in London, were unfavourably received. The boldness of the next scheme which he conceived, and the mingled adroitness and determination with which he carried it through, afford a better measure, perhaps, than any other incident of his career, of the really remarkable qualities he possessed.

[1] In the list of bankrupts published in the *Gentleman's Magazine* for October 1773 occurs the name William Bolts, of Harpur Street, Red Lion Square, merchant.

BOOK II

CHAPTER I

MR BOLTS AND THE EMPRESS MARIA THERESA

EARLY in 1774 Mr Bolts had made his way to Vienna, and had succeeded in establishing himself as a "persona grata" at the Court of the Empress Maria Theresa, representing himself as a loyal subject of the Empire, to which a considerable part of the Netherlands then owed allegiance. Two years later he revisited Vienna and gained the confidence of the Empress to such an extent that she made him a Lieut.-Colonel in the Imperial Army, and placed him in command of an expedition destined to attempt the task of wresting from the English Company some part of the lucrative commerce of the East Indies.

Rumours of this design were soon afloat, and advices from numerous correspondents in Southern Europe began to arrive at Leadenhall Street. There was at this period a close working alliance between the East India Company and the Foreign Office, and the earliest intimation which the Company received was contained in a letter from Lisbon addressed to the Secretary of State for Foreign Affairs, dated the 4th of April 1776:

"Mr William Bolts, some time a servant of the English East India Company, and probably known to your Lordship, both by his contest with them, and by his publication on their affairs in East India, arrived here a few days ago in an English vessel of near 1100 tons burthen, lately known by the name of the *Earl of Lincoln*. He cleared out from London on an English vessel, manned by above sixty British seamen, under the command of Captain Samuel

Butler, almost all of whom Mr Bolts has already dismissed from his ship, as will endeavour that he shall the others before he leaves this harbour. It is hardly doubtful that he is bound on a voyage to East India, pursuant to agreement with the Court of Vienna, and he entered this port under Imperial colours, but he asserts that his destination is up the Streights of Gibraltar. I understand indeed that he is bound immediately to Leghorn, but that he is there to find more ships ready, and to proceed with them to India, accompanied by a Frenchman [1] of the name of Ryan, who goes second in authority.

This man has parts and eloquence; and if, during a visit he made to Vienna two years ago, he has succeeded to excite that court to new attempts of an East India trade, though they will probably end as the last did, [2] and he in such case be inevitably the victim of it, yet his industry and intimate knowledge of that country may enable him to do no slight mischief there."

This warning was supplemented by a letter from His Majesty's Envoy at Florence, addressed to the Foreign Office, dated the 20th of April 1776, a copy of which was sent to the Directors:

" I think it my duty to acquaint your Lordship that two Danish and one Dutch ship lately arrived at Leghorn from Trieste, loaden with cannon, balls, powder, musquets, and flints, with many articles that are mentioned in the enclosed lists, all of which effects were consignable to a Mr Frank, a Hamburg Merchant there, and have been deposited in his warehouses. Mr Frank is now at Florence, with two gentlemen from Anvers, Baron Proly and his nephew Count Proly, who are the directors of these cargoes and had frequent conferences with the Great Duke [3] about them. On board each of those ships from Trieste were a few Austrian soldiers, all Lutherans, who are now at Leghorn. I have been assured by a person in the utmost confidence, that the object of the plan now in question is purely of a commercial nature with China, set on foot by Messrs Proly before mentioned, and at present carried into execution at

---

[1] From an extract quoted below, page 139, it appears that he had been in the counting-house of an English firm at Lisbon.

[2] The Ostend Company, which had enjoyed the patronage and support of the Court of Vienna, collapsed in 1734. The States-General having first abandoned it, the Emperor signed at Paris on the 20th of May 1727 the treaty by which the Charter of the Ostend Company was suspended for seven years, owing to the combined pressure of the hostility of Great Britain, France, Spain, and Holland. It had commenced operations, though not yet as an organised Company, as far back as the year 1718.

[3] The Grand Duke of Tuscany, the Archduke Leopold, younger brother of the Emperor Joseph II.

the expense of the Empress Queen, but with a view, in case this first expedition should succeed, to form a regular Company to carry on a trade with those parts. The same person says that a large Merchant ship had been purchased in England, which is soon expected at Leghorn, on which the effects from Trieste are to be embarked, and the ship under Austrian colours to sail directly for the coast of China. I have been further assured, that the Empress Queen has declared that she would remove any obstacle to this establishment which might arise from any Foreign Power; and the Grand Duke has said on this occasion, that in consideration of the present rebellion in America, proper security would be given in England, that the arms and ammunition to be put on board the vessel at Leghorn should not be carried to the rebels there."

Later communications from Florence of the 2nd of July and the 28th of September 1776 state that Mr Bolts has been in conference with the Great Duke, and that the *Florentine Gazette* has openly declared that the ship " belongs to a company erected in Germany, to carry on a commerce between Trieste and the coast of Coromandel," and to establish a factory there:

"The ship is now preparing with the utmost expedition for the voyage, and is to be escorted to a certain distance by one of the Great Duke's frigates, to protect it against the Barbary Corsairs." . . . "The loading of the ship is very rich, and consists chiefly of . . . side and fire arms for 30,000 men, cannon of different sizes, powder, . . . copper, steel, paper, cord, cochineal, cables, woollen clothes and stuffs, silk stockings, wine, and Spanish dollars. Orders have been given to insure for £65,000 at 10 to 12 per cent. premium from Leghorn to the coast of Coromandel, Bengal, Malabar, China, and the Gulf of Persia, and for the return."

On the 24th of December the Directors wrote to Warren Hastings and his colleagues, enclosing extracts from the letters just quoted, together with two letters dated the 13th November and the 23rd December from Madeira, and giving instructions how to deal with the members of the expedition when it reached India. They were to boycott all the members of the expeditionary force, and to arrest and bring to England all the British subjects who belonged to it.

EXTRACT OF ADVICES FROM MADEIRA. NO. 1

"The ship *Joseph and Theresa*[1] commanded by William Bolts arrived here the 24th October, and sailed for India the 1st instant. A Tuscan (or Imperial) ship has been lately here, bound for the East Indies; she was to have carried about 100 pipes of wines, but the Government here would not admit of her taking any more than five or six for use in their voyage, for reasons best known to themselves."

EXTRACT OF ADVICES FROM MADEIRA. NO. 2

"On the 29th May last arrived here the Brigantine *Bland*, John Hardy Master, from London with a quantity of cordage (said to be about 30 tons) which was stored in the Custom House, to be reshipped on board the *Joseph and Tereza*, on her arrival; and in said Brig[ne] *Bland* came passenger Mr Cohl (some time since a merchant in Lisbon) who staid here until the coming of the *Joseph and Tereza*, and proceeded in her, but in what capacity cannot with any certainty inform you; the cordage of the *Bland* was not admitted to be reshipped by the Government of this island, but still lays in the Custom House.

On the 24th October came into this port the ship *Joseph and Teresa*, commanded by Captain William Bolts from Leghorn, this ship we heard had been the *Lincoln*, East India-man, and, to all outward appearance, did not carry any greater number of guns than when in the English service, which was twenty-six, or capable of mounting thirty-two; her complement of seamen and soldiers we have not had it in our power to obtain a certainty of; but she appeared full of people, and therefore we compute she had not less than ninety or one hundred mariners, and sixty or seventy soldiers; for soldiers we saw performing their exercises on board the ship. On board the *Joseph and Tereza* was a Mr Bryan[2] (formerly a clerk

---

[1] The *Earl of Lincoln* had been rechristened by this name.

[2] He appears as Mr "Ryan" in an extract quoted above. Among the Miscellaneous documents relating to this period at the India Office is a letter from Mr W. G. Farmer, a Bombay official, dated January 1798, strongly recommending a Mr Murdock Brown to the Directors for employment in the Company's service on the Malabar coast. He represented him as having rendered invaluable assistance to Sir Ralph Abercrombie during the war with Tipu, also to Governor Duncan, as well as to himself, and stated that he had been originally taken out to India "by the famous Mr Bolts, who ... employed him chiefly on the Mallabar coast." When Mr Bolts's affairs became involved, Mr Brown seems to have settled at Mahé, "where he was permitted to trade and where he derived further security from his diploma of Imperial Consul." I am inclined to suspect that this Mr Murdock Brown may be no other than the "Ryan" or "Bryan" of these Foreign Office communications.

in the Counting-house of Messrs Maynes of Lisbon[1]), this gentleman we heard was the first super-cargo : there was likewise a Mr Paul who had been in business as a merchant at Lisbon, his station on the expedition we do not know. In company of the *Joseph and Teresa* came an English brigantine named the *Lyon*, George Culverwill master (from Leghorn), this brig^{ne} we understand has six cables and a quantity of copper on board to be reshipped on the *Joseph and Tereza* which the Government here would not permit to be done in their port ; the Brigantine therefore sailed in company from this, with the *Joseph and Tereza* the 1st November ; to what part of India is the destination of the *Joseph and Tereza* we cannot learn ; neither have we heard anything respecting any other ships upon the expedition. The cargo on board the *Joseph and Tereza* was only mentioned here in general terms, 'Goods for the India Market,' and altho' she was to have taken in about 100 pipes of Madeira wine here, the Government would not admit her receiving on board a greater quantity than six or seven pipes for use on the voyage ; the wines were to have been laden by a Domingos Mendez Viana, who is administrator for the farmer general at Lisbon of the Customs here. *P.S.*—I have just learnt that Mr William Bolts was chief Manager, Captain, and a Lieut.-Colonel, in His Imperial Majesty's service, and, as such, he produced his patent, and there were fifty Imperial soldiers on board the ship only."

EXTRACT FROM LETTER FROM COURT OF THE 24TH DECEMBER 1776

"We are informed from unquestionable authority that an enterprize of trade is in agitation by Mr William Bolts (formerly in our service in Bengal) under Imperial colours and the protection of the Queen of Hungary, in a large ship late the *Earl of Lincoln* now named the *Joseph and Theresa* which towards the end of June imported[2] at Leghorn from Lisbon, where beside considerable quantities of Goods before shipped, ordnance, ammunition, and all kinds of military stores to a great amount were received on board, with a

---

[1] Perhaps the same firm with whom Mr Bolts had been as a youth.

[2] Other instances of this curious usage of the word "import" are the following :

"The Honble. Company's ships *Valentine*, *Houghton*, and *Stormont* have imported here the first on the 25th ult. and the two later on the 10th instant." (Letter from the President and Consul of Fort St George, Madras, to the President and Council of Fort William, Calcutta, dated the 13th of July 1777. "The accompanying list will shew you the several ships that have imported here from India and China in the course of this season." (Letter from Court of the 11th November 1768.)

very valuable proportion of merchandize, consisting principally of iron, copper, and steel brought thither by two Danish and a Dutch ship from Trieste, and as the *Florentine Gazette* published by authority avows "belonging to a Company erected in Germany to carry on commerce between Trieste and the coast of Choromandel, where the House of Austria means to establish a new factory. We are also given to understand that a number of Austrian soldiers, Lutherans, were to be embarked at Leghorn on board the said ship, which left that port the 25th of September last with her consort an English brigantine laden with provisions for the voyage, and that both were from the Canary Islands to continue their course to the coast of Choromandel. For more minute particulars of this expedition you are referred to the accompanying extracts of a correspondence concerning it.

It remains for us by the present opportunity in the strongest manner to recommend to your serious consideration, either separately or conjunctively with our other presidencies, to pursue the most effectual means that can be fully justified to counteract and defeat the same; observing at the same time that this commerce is not contrary to any treaty at present subsisting. It will be particularly necessary to counteract this scheme in the beginning, because if the adventurers meet with but indifferent success in this first essay, it may discourage them from future attempts. If their design to settle shall be in the neighbourhood of your presidency, we particularly rely on your weight and efforts with the Country Powers to render the scheme abortive.

We further especially recommend the stopping commercial and other intercourse of our covenanted servants, and all under our protection, with the persons who conduct this expedition, or are concerned therein, and to prevent the latter from being furnished by any persons subject to our authority, with money, goods, stores, or any other assistance, conducive to the execution of their plan, and in case of the breach of any orders issued in this behalf, it is left to you to shew a resentment adequate to the nature of the offence.

As there are sufficient reasons to conclude several British subjects are employed in the expedition, who are by the laws of this Kingdom now in force liable to be arrested and brought to Great Britain, if found in the East Indies without our license, we direct that you put such laws in force.

You will receive by us or our agents by every opportunity in the course of the season what further intelligence shall offer on this subject, that such measures may be taken as shall appear expedien in consequence thereof."

In the autumn of 1777 the Governor-General and Consul received from the Directors the following additional particulars contained in a letter from Leghorn, dated the 21st March :

"You are probably apprized that a Company at Ostend have laden an Imperial ship for Coromandel under the direction of Mr Bolts, which left this place in October last, to the amount of piastres 40,000 in coral of different qualities but of an inferior sort, as he was pressed for time, and could not procure such as he should have taken. He took a large quantity of brandies (Rosils), chests of arms, silver, copper, steel, 200 bales of our paper, which is cheap and fit for the India Market, ophium, cutlery, iron work, silk stockings, thread, linen cloth, sathies[1] and Florence silks. The greater part of the above is our produce. Mr Bolts in forming this cargo run to a needless and even extravagant expense, and paid the officers and sailors very largely and without economy."

On the 7th of July 1777 the Governor-General and Council, in accordance with the instructions received from the Directors, issued a boycotting notice, circulated in Madras and in Bombay as well as in Bengal, against

"Mr William Bolts, late a servant of the Hon. East India Company, who is now on his way to India in a ship called the *Joseph and Theresa*." . . . "The Honble. the Court of Directors judging it expedient to guard against any injury which their commerce may suffer by this undertaking, have thought proper to forbid their covenanted servants and all others under their protection to hold any commercial or other intercourse with him or any of the agents or seamen of the said ship, or to supply them directly or indirectly with money, goods, stores, or any other assistance which may conduce to the execution of this plan." . . . "Notice is therefore given that a strict observance of this prohibition is expected and required."

On the 16th of July the President and Council of Bombay sent in a report on the progress of the *Joseph and Theresa*. The relevant portion of their report ran :

"By a country vessel from Delagoa we learn that a ship under

---

[1] For an explanation of this obscure word I am indebted to Lieut.-Col. P. R. T. Gurdon, who has suggested that it is the Hindustani and Bengali 'sáth' or 'sáthi,' sixty. If this is correct, it means 'sixties,' a fine count of cotton goods.

Austrian colours and with a very rich cargo arrived there in the month of April and had been run on shore in endeavouring to bring her into the river. Mr Bolts, formerly on the Bengal establishment, was principal owner and commander of this ship under a commission from the Emperor, and had taken in his cargo at Leghorn and Trieste. His associate Mr Ryan arrived here on the above-mentioned country vessel, and now proceeds to Bengal on the *Hastings* snow, which makes me conjecture that the ship is destined to your side of India, if she can be got off, and we therefore think it proper to give you this intelligence."

In a later report of the 22nd of August they mention that the vessel on which Mr Ryan took passage was forced into Damaun by stress of weather, and conclude that she will not be able to proceed on her voyage for some time.

In spite of these mishaps, however, Mr Bolts ultimately succeeded in bringing the *Joseph and Theresa* to the port of Surat.

CHAPTER II

MR BOLTS AND THE CHEVALIER DE ST LUBIN:
INTRIGUES AT POONA

IN their General Letter to the Directors of the 30th of November 1777, the Bombay Government announce the arrival of Mr Bolts at Surat:

" Mr Bolts in the Austrian ship *Joseph and Theresa* to our great surprise arrived at Surat Bar the 5th September. An extract of your commands dated 21st February had been previously sent thither and the Chief and Council in consequence thereof and of the further orders we sent upon receiving advice of the ship's arrival, exerted themselves so much and with the assistance of the Nabob's influence threw so many obstacles in his way that Mr Bolts found himself unable to transact any business there and sailed away for Gogo.[1] The Chiefs at Surat and Broach will use every justifiable method to prevent his meeting with success, and we learn he has not yet been able to sell any part of his cargo, but that he had sent to the Pundit of Ahmedabad to whom Gogo is subordinate offering him a present of Rs. 25,000 annually in lieu of customs, provided he will permit him to establish a Factory and carry on a trade there. He has since proceeded to Poonah to negotiate this business himself, but we shall exert our little influence with the Durbar to defeat this scheme and you may be assured that no justifiable or legal efforts shall be left untried to frustrate the projects of these adventurers.

We have sent the most strict injunctions to all your subordinate settlements to have no commercial or other intercourse with the persons concerned in this ship and to prevent any investments whatever being made for them.

The commander of a country vessel trading to Delagoa has advised his owners here that Mr Bolts asserted a right to that country by virtue of a grant from the African king to her Imperial Majesty and had left ten men and some guns to maintain possession. We have got a copy of Mr Bolts' letter to the above-mentioned

---
[1] A port in the Ahmadabad district of Bombay.

commander asserting this right which shall be sent by the *Hawke*, and in consequence thereof he pulled down the English colours and a house the captain had erected there for the purpose of carrying on his trade.

The Chief and Council at Surat advise us that the cargo of the Austrian ship consisted of iron, copper, steel, cochineal, saffron, a large quantity of ordnance and warlike stores, and some jewellry, to the amount of about five Lacs of rupees."

In the same letter mention is made of the intrigues of a French adventurer, the Chevalier de St Lubin, at Poona, with whom Mr Bolts was intimately associated soon after this date. In a note penned by Warren Hastings on the Peshwah's Government in February 1778, he remarks :

" Nannah Furneess (one of the members of the Government) is about 50 years: has the sole direction of all current affairs and aspires to the first command. . . . He has given protection to the Chevalier de St Lubin and Mr Bolts."[1]

---

[1] A Bombay civilian named Farmer, writing from Poona on the 11th November 1777, gave a very unfavourable account of St Lubin : "This St Lubin is a most perfect adventurer, and I believe has cheated even the Ministry of France in this business. He introduced himself to the confidence of M. de Sartine, as to Indian matters, by a memorial he presented relative to this country . . ." in which ". . . he has made himself the generalissimo at one time of Hyder's army . . . the constant companion of the children of the Raja of the Mahrattas . . . in short he had not in the world a better friend than the Raja. . . . I have examined all the Frenchmen, with whom we have yet had connection. . . . They are all in such a situation with respect to M. St Lubin that it is the first wish of their lives that he may prove a counterfeit, and not be supported by the Ministry of France ; for in fact their lives may perhaps depend on Lubin's reality." St Lubin did actually attempt the life of M. de Corcelle, a follower ; the latter sought refuge with the English. In a letter dated 3rd January 1778 William Mackintosh gives a somewhat more flattering account of St Lubin : "A person without any visible fortune, who by a long unsettled residence in India has acquired an uncommon knowledge of the customs, manners, policy, trade, etc.," of the inhabitants of India, Native and European. ". . . From the station of a private soldier in Mauritius, by genius, activity, address, fluency of speech, and withal a considerable share of assurance, he has risen to his present eminence. He ingratiated himself very much with some of the Directors of the East India Company, and since the suspension of their charter, he has acquired the favour and confidence of M. de Sartine in so high a degree, that if his abilities had not been thought more usefully employed in a walk of life not so public, he would have been appointed to the Govern-

The Chevalier de St Lubin had arrived at Poona in May 1777, with a letter and presents from the King of France,[1] and quickly ingratiated himself with Nana Farnavis, the influential supporter of the infant Peshwa, Madhu Rao Narayana, against the claims of Raghuba, who after the murder of his nephew Narayana Rao, the fifth Peshwa, had been recognised as successor to the Mahratta throne by the Bombay Government under the Treaty of Surat. Nana Farnavis made an agreement with St Lubin by which there was to be a close alliance between the Mahrattas and the King of France, the former conceding to France the immediate use and future possession of the port of Chaul, thirty miles south of Bombay, while the latter was to support the Mahrattas with a military force and with stores.

On the 10th of May 1777 the Bombay Government reported to Bengal that as a result of this intrigue M. de St Lubin had already written to the French Ministry to despatch a force to Poona to the assistance of Nana Farnavis, and repeated their urgent pleas for the alliance with Raghuba as absolutely essential to British interests.

The majority of the Supreme Council had disallowed the Treaty of Surat and substituted the Treaty of Purandar in 1776, by which Raghuba was to be abandoned. But Hornby, the Bombay Governor, a strong and able ruler, had refused to obey the orders

ment of Pondicherry. . . . He has lately been dignified with a military order, and is now invested with the sole direction of two large trading ships on the coast of Malabar, where his address, his knowledge, and his ready access to Hyder Ally, and the Maratta tribes, are very likely to attain the object of his employers, the re-establishment of their trade and the resumption of their charter."

[1] He brought also 15,000 rejected muskets, sold to him from the royal arsenals very cheap, and a varied cargo, including a number of buttons for the uniforms of the native troops that might be raised for the purpose of the alliance. These buttons had the device of the Fleur-de-Lys in a crescent, M. St Lubin evidently supposing that the Mahrattas were Muhammadans!

K

of the majority and appealed to the Directors and to the King. The Directors promptly approved of the Treaty of Surat, and thus vindicated Hornby. But even Francis and his colleagues now had their eyes opened by the intrigues of the French to the unwisdom of their previous action in upsetting the policy of the Bombay Government contrary to the counsel of Warren Hastings; henceforward the Supreme Government, the Directors, and the Bombay Government were at one on the necessity of breaking through the Treaty of Purandar and supporting Raghuba's claims.

In April 1778 Warren Hastings and his colleagues informed the Directors of the presence at Mahé of the French Governor-General, M. de Bellecombes, in connection with St Lubin's intrigues, as they believed, and expressed their fears of a French attempt to seize Chaul with the assistance of the Mahrattas. The following extract from a letter dated the 12th of July 1778 from M. de Bellecombes at Pondicherry to M. Chevalier, Governor of Chandernagore, shows what was the spirit animating the representatives of the French nation at this period, and what good ground there was for the apprehensions expressed by the Bengal Government :

"Il seroit bon de prévenir de ma part les Marattes du Kateck et du Berar des dispositions des Anglois relativement à la guerre qui paroit inevitable, que j'écris a ceux de Poonah que c'est le moment de se réunir tous pour écraser cette nation ambitieuse qui a déja fait des pertes considérables en l'Amérique qu'elle cherchera à reparer en subjugant tous les Princes de l'Inde."

A flood of light is thrown upon the intrigues of M. de St Lubin and upon the doings of Mr Bolts by the contents of an intercepted packet despatched by M. Anquetil de Briancourt, French consul at Surat, to M. de Sartines, Minister of Marine, at Paris, which fell into the hands of the Bombay Government and was by them transmitted to the Directors. The following extracts show very clearly the designs of the French agents and their close relations with Mr Bolts:

(1) From M. Anquetil de Briancourt, French Consul at Surat, to the Chevalier de St Lubin at Poona, dated Surat the 20th June 1777.

". . . I am so much observed here by the Nabob and the English, that I dare not risk a letter. . . . This is put into your hands by M. le Roy, a Captain of a ship, one of those who was with M. de Bougainville in his voyage round the world. . . . Accept, Sir, the very sincere congratulations which I offer you on your title of Minister from the King at the Court of Poonah. I have received with great pleasure the agreeable news which you gave me in your letter of the 11th of May. Your arrival in this part of the world makes a great impression on the people of the country and confounds the English very much.

You are come to Poonah in very good time; that Court wanted your assistance to oblige the English to keep all the articles of their last treaty of peace. They will be constrained to do it, if Chaoul, which your good offices have procured for the French, is well supported by the nation and the Court of Poonah. I have certain information that the English watch for the moment when Chaoul shall be defenceless, to send Ragonaut Row and his little army supported by their troops, to drive the French from thence; but I think your residence at Poonah will render all their attempts fruitless, and that they will find at last that the French nation has at present persons at the head of their affairs in this country, capable of making them retreat as quickly as they have advanced to conquer almost all India. It is said further that the English have an intention of seizing Bassein, and that they are making preparations to that end. This news is likely to be true, because in case of a war Bassein will become necessary to them to secure and maintain the intercourse between Bombay and Surat; an intercourse which would, to their great prejudice, be interrupted if Bassein should fall into our hands. As the English reckon on an approaching war in Europe, all their steps at present are only preparative to putting their fortresses in a state of security; but they are too numerous in this country, to be all preserved. The three most important on this coast at present are Bombay, Surat, and Baroche, but the two latter cannot hold out long, as soon as Bombay, the first fortress, shall be attacked.

If you desire any explanation respecting Surat, M. de Roy will satisfy you. . . . If you shall approve what he tells you on my behalf, I am ready to correspond with you for the good of the service." . . . The Persian servant who accompanies M. le Roy "should bring me your answer, as well as that to M. Rouveau, Commander of a detachment at present at Surat . . . a very honest man, above all an excellent *Frenchman*. . . . He is able to augment your forces by the junction which he can effect of a number of French scattered here and there on the sea coast. . . .

I do not ask you, Sir, what are your operations at Poonah. Your capacity answers me for the success of your negotiations at that Court. The King could not make a better choice in naming you his Minister there; and the English tremble here; but I should be very happy that you would confirm to me the great advantages which the nation already derives from your negotiations at Poonah. It is said here that Mr Mostyn the Counsellor of Bombay cannot obtain an audience of the Princess Nana,[1] that you are daily and well received by her, that you have an hundred Europeans with you, who are encamped within ten leagues of the capital, where the Court is at present, that she has granted to you a jaghire of 5 lacks of rupees from the neighbourhood of Chaoul—that you have obtained leave to build a fort there, and that according to your convention made with the Marattas you are to receive three ships of war and some troops at Chaoul.

If all this news be true, the English do not tremble for nothing; and the Nabob of Surat may in a little time repent of the two affronts he offered me at the instigation of the English in the months of March and April last.

I beg, Sir, you will impart to me the agreeable confirmation of your success. It is two years since I began to negotiate with the Court of Poonah by means of Govine Ragonath. I have had fair promises made to me, which were to be executed as soon as the French should appear in force at Poonah. Divine Providence seconding your zeal has conducted you thither. What can I desire more for the benefit of the nation? I have therefore given up this correspondence, the channel of which I informed you of by the few lines which mentioned the money I had of yours. If you have any need of my services at Poonah and Chaoul, have the goodness to command them. I doubt whether there are provisions of grain and of other sorts at Chaoul. I can furnish you with them from Surat, which the English, with great reason, look upon as their magazine for provisions.

Chaoul will certainly hurt the Settlement of Surat, which has only the duties to support it. If however this new fort should correspond well with Surat, I may perhaps be able to draw from it

---

[1] Gunga Bai, widow of Narayan Rao and mother of the young Peshwa, appears to be meant. See below, page 152.

the means of improving this Settlement. You will consider, Sir, what you are to think on this point ; communicate your ideas to me, and I will impart mine to you, which when united cannot but contribute essentially to the good of the nation on this side of India.

As I presume in all your negotiations at Poonah and your operations at Chaoul you act in concert with M. de Bellecombes,[1] I should not suffer you to remain ignorant of the survey I have caused to be made of Goga.[2] . . . I think the French may derive great advantages from that port. Then its situation is such that the commerce of all the neighbouring great cities, even of Surat itself, will flow to Goga, if we are in possession of it. This city which might be made a very important port is at present inhabited only by Mariners. The Court of Poonah will not refuse you the cession of this place if you ask it. If we fail in this, the English will have Goga sooner.

An idea has lately struck me which, if realized, would be advantageous to the nation and release me from a great deal of trouble and uneasiness. It is this ; it being much to be feared that the new acquisition of Chaoul, excellent as it is in itself, will entirely overthrow the Settlement of Surat, and as this Settlement is of use to the nation, but having at present nothing but the duties for its support, it must fall, as its revenues will fail by the establishment of Chaoul ; the means then of supporting this tottering Settlement are in your hands, Sir. The most trifling jaghire would render this service to the nation. Having procured information on the subject I have discovered Danmans, a large town, at four leagues distance from here, and which is at the head of Surat River by the side of the Road belonging to the Court of Poonah. Its revenue is inconsiderable, but however it will be sufficient for me to defray the charges of this Settlement. The jaghire or revenue of Danmans and its environs is from twenty to twenty-five thousand rupees a year ; all charges deducted and sundry distributions made, fifteen thousand at least would remain for us. This perwannah of Danmans is of so little consequence to the Princess Nana, that I think she will grant it you very willingly, but it is very important to the nation, because by this means the Settlement of Surat will always subsist independent of its trade, whether much or little. Besides, the situation of a place at the mouth of Surat River would render us, in case of war, masters of all the commerce of that City. The third advantage M. le Roy will demonstrate to you is that Danmans is the most favourable place to form a descent against Surat, in case it were thought proper. What will not the French nation owe you, Sir, if by your negotiations at Poonah you procure this triple advantage ? And as it likewise tends to economy, the minister cannot but render you

---

[1] Governor-General of the French possessions in India, at Pondicherry.
[2] See page 143, note.

his thanks. . . . I cannot conclude my letter without imparting to you a most essential observation. If war has been declared in Europe as the last Gazettes give us reason to fear, you have in your own hands the means of furnishing the Marattas with a sufficient reason to attack Surat. The fortress of Surat at present occupied by the English depends originally on the Government of Ragypourry. It was a Siddy[1] of Ragypourry[2] who was in possession of it in 1759 and who was driven out by the English that same year. The Maratta Government has great claims on Ragypourry. This place is near Chaoul, nothing therefore can be easier than to seize it, and afterwards to demand of the Nabob and the English at Surat to account for the duties and jaghires of the Fort, revenues which should return immediately to Ragypourry. Their refusal will determine the expedition against Surat. This plan, presented by you and adopted by the Marattas, would not be difficult to put in execution at the first declaration of war, and I shall then exert all the local knowledge I have of this city, and the desire I have of serving my nation, which would lead me to seize with ardour this opportunity of demonstrating my zeal. Pray, Sir, take care this letter falls into no other hands than your own. I am sure you must see the consequences of it. . . .

P.S.—I forgot to tell you, Sir, that two pattamars[3] coming from Poonah were stopped at Surat about six weeks ago. Among several letters belonging to the merchants of Surat I am afraid there was one addressed to me, and that the whole packet was immediately dispatched to Bombay, since which I hear nothing further of it. . . . We cannot observe too much circumspection in our reciprocal correspondence. You have nothing to fear where you are, but M. le Roy will tell you how I am day and night exposed to every species of insult since the French have been at Chaoul. I hope this distressing situation will not last long. . . ."

(2) From M. Anquetil de Briancourt to M. de St Lubin, 1st August 1777.

. . . .

"The report you have heard is false; I am, it is true, closely watched by the English and the Nabob, but I am not at all concerned at that. The affair at the stairs arose from a blunder of Mr Day's who has behaved to me like a mere Quixote, during the absence of Mr Boddam the English Chief, who was then at Baroche. I am intimately connected with the latter, I often dine with him, and he does the same with me. . . . Notwithstanding the desire I

---

[1] Chief. Properly a title applied to African Muhammadans.
[2] Rajapur.   [3] Express messengers.

have to see and confer with you, I doubt of my having that happiness. The English Company have given express orders to all their Settlements that you must not set foot in them. This proscription will render an interview rather difficult, but not impossible."

(3) From the same to the same, 4th September 1777.

"I beg your acceptance of my sincere congratulations on the good success of your mission, and am much obliged to you for the explanation you have given me on that subject. The treaty of alliance and commerce concluded with the Court of Poonah will do you much honour at Court, and will afford infinite satisfaction to M. de Sartines, and will procure considerable advantage to France, if she will make the most of the circumstance and will afford you support in time. The Minister is already informed on this point; I wrote him in April last, on account of the arrival of the French at Chaoul and the Embassy to Poonah, but as I was then ignorant that it was you who were arrived in the *Sartine*, I was not able to give the Minister any explanation, nor inform him of the names of the persons at the head of this undertaking which I had placed to the account of the Consolante, not knowing neither of the arrival of the *Sartine*. . . .

The English at Surat have as yet no intelligence of your treaty of alliance. I am on too good a footing with the English chief for him to have concealed it from me, had he known it; but I have not mentioned it to him, because in short he is an Englishman, and that haughty nation being too powerful at Surat ridicule everything which is not done or supported by force of arms. Therefore I rather wish the English should tell me of it themselves. I shall then discover the impression this news makes on their minds. They have already told me it was impossible the Marrattas should be allied to the French, by virtue of an ancient treaty made between them, by which the Marrattas promised to form no other alliance with any European nation. The English are preparing themselves at Bombay; sometimes we are told it is in order to conduct Ragoba to Chaoul or Bassein, sometimes it is to conquer Guzurat, to enthrone him at Poonah; for my own part I think it is to put themselves in a posture of defence against the French in time of war or in case of a sudden attack.

I am sorry the jaghires are not in the agreement, but I am sure you will easily find means to annex them to it, if the troops promised to you arrive—without knowing anything of your mission, I was very importunate in my request to M. de Sartines to send speedily some troops or ships of war to support the operations of the French at Chaoul . . . and give more credit to their negotiations at the

Court of Poonah; at the same time pointed out to him the consequences of delay. You see I have furthered your views without your having any knowledge of it, and without my knowing I was acting for you; in which I think myself very fortunate. Have we, Sir, a right of a Settlement or Residence, and a right of a flag at Chaoul or Bassein? These two prerogatives would make me very happy, if the Nabob of Surat, at the instigation of the English, should drive me to extremities. If the French are privileged and treated with respect in one of these two places, I should prefer Chaoul from that circumstance. With your assistance I shall know how to make the Nabob of Surat and the English themselves repent of their ill behaviour to me, but we are not yet come to that. As I know the Nabob is under the yoke, and that at the bottom he has a regard for me, I shall remain quiet till the last extremity.

It is very unfortunate for us that the Princess of Poonah is dead. I fear this accident may disconcert your operations; the English say here, she was poisoned, and that it is actually publicly known at Poonah that the young prince is a suppositious child or a natural son of Nana Pharvis which the Princess had by him; they add that it was the Minister who gave her poison, because she was with child, and he did not wish his connexion with her to be known.[1] Pray inform me of the truth of this.

Our interview, Sir, is become necessary, for the reasons you give me, and I have arranged my affairs so as to fix it at Daman. . . . I must prepare relays of palanqueens every ten leagues and travel night and day. I will give you advice in my next letter of the time when I can take this secret journey. . . .

You tell me that you engage warmly as to Damans and Goga, and that you do not lose sight of the Seiddy of Ragapourry. I attend with impatience the success of your negotiations as to Damans. As that little jaghire belongs of right to Satara Bapore, if they wish you well in the smallest degree, as Nana Pharnis does, he will easily grant it to me at your intercession, and as this place commands the Road of Surat, it is a strong hold from whence we may draw succours very advantageous to the Marrattas themselves. The affair if represented by you in this point of view cannot fail of success. . . . It would require a volume to tell you my grievances from the English; I postpone that business till our meeting. . . . I am at present so short of cash, that it is the sale of the merchandize remaining in my hands on which I subsist; and I have for these eight months advanced my own money for the support of this Settlement."

---

[1] Gunga Bai poisoned herself, to conceal her intrigue with Nana Farnavis. The young Peshwa was probably legitimate, though the Bombay Government believed otherwise.

(4) From the same to the same, 7th September 1777.

"The English who are very uneasy at your negotiations have spread a report here of your death, and have even sent to tell me of it. I answered that it was talked of 15 days ago at Poonah, that I had taken my flight from Surat; that the falsity of this news effectually proved that of the report respecting you, also that it certainly proceeded from the same source, which I was endeavouring to discover. . . . This deceitful nation, for at least they are so at present to you and me, have made some other news to be believed since yesterday, which I credit no more than the first, it is this: they say that Mr Mostyn the English Counsellor is just come back from Poonah to Bombay with Nana Pharnis. This minister of that Court, say they, accompanied him to offer Ragobah the throne of Poonah, where he is expected in order to ascend it and expel the young Prince. As you tell me in your letter of the 17th of last month that there begins to be a misunderstanding, I am led to believe that whenever Mr Mostyn returns to Bombay, it will be because he and his suite are driven from Poonah. Pray give me the key to this enigma. They report also that the Commander of the *Sartine* is come to Bombay on business, but that he was refused admittance there. . . ."

(5) From the same to the same, 13th September 1777.

. . . .

"This will be put into your hands by Mr Bolts, Lieutenant-Colonel in Her Imperial Majesty's Service and Commander of the ship *Theresa*. Half an hour's conversation with him will acquaint you with what concerns him. I think you will find in this sensible worthy gentleman everything necessary to give your operations more vigour by his uniting himself with you. Perhaps you may not be displeased with such an assistance, and at having the opportunity of convincing the Empress-Queen of the zeal every good French-man has for her service. Similar misfortunes produce a friendship between the most indifferent persons. Mr Bolts is looked upon by the English in the same light as you are. The Company have given the strictest orders to annoy his ship and even his person as much as possible. This honest Commander and his wife began to feel the effects of this proscription at Surat, where I parried the blow as well as I was able. As Mr Bolts has been second at Benares in the English service, and as his disagreement with the Council of Calcutta has covered the Company with confusion, so far that the Ministry have been obliged to send a new Administration to Bengal, that Company pursue him by their agents in India, and will pursue him to the last. This was his crime, Sir, and it is yours;[1] but two men of talents like yours united may give the English some trouble and which they will be much afraid of when they hear of your meeting. I trust that great advantages will result from it to the two nations, and it is that which determined me so strongly to engage Mr Bolts to see you. I am persuaded you will be pleased with it. As you are united by the same views, this reciprocal communication of ideas cannot but be of infinite service to our affairs. Besides you will be pleased to be particularly acquainted with this brave and worthy man whose reputation is established, and who on account of his own merits needs no letter of recommendation from me. I think I shall have your thanks for procuring you such a visit. Pray do not let me remain ignorant of the good arising from it. I have nothing new to inform you from this country, and Mr Bolts can tell you nothing more of Surat than of politics and the French garden. The latter place is looked upon by the Nabob as the Lazaretto of the Imperial ship, and filled with people who might bring the plague into the city, if they were allowed to enter it, and the English fearing the contagion, and very zealous for good government, have also wisely foreseen it. . . ."

(6) From the same to the same, 2nd October 1777.

.   .   .   .

"In my last I forgot to inform you of the arrival of an Imperial vessel in this Road, commanded by Mr Bolts. The English have thwarted him so that he has not been able to unlade anything, and had it not been for the hospitality I showed him, I know not what would have become of him. Fearing the Coup de Vent de la Saint François[2] he is gone to Goga, where my letters have procured him a good reception from the people of the country. As I am treating with the Nabob to secure his trade here, he will return to this Road

---

[1] M. de St Lubin had imposed upon the English Government at Madras before he returned to France and gained the ear of the French Ministry.

[2] *i.e.* "the autumn monsoon"; *cf.* page 161. "La St François," the Festival of St Francis, can properly be understood in French to refer only to St Francis of Assisi, whose festival is on the 4th of October, two days after this letter was written, and not to St Francis Xavier, whose festival is on the 3rd of December. But the writer seems to have connected the phrase, whether purposely or inadvertently, with St Francis Xavier, who encountered a terrible three days' storm on a voyage to Goa in the autumn of 1551. The legendary fame of the latter saint, who preached Christianity in the Portuguese colonies on the Malabar coast with great success in the first half of the sixteenth century, was strong enough at that time to make such a confusion of sanctities possible.

after the bad monsoon, which does not last above a fortnight; but the Nabob must be tractable to admit of that. I doubt it, as Bombay keeps him under the yoke.   Mr Bolts was formerly second at Benaries in the English service; as he laid open to the Public the infamous administration of the Company in Bengal, he is pursued by them wherever he can be found; but under the auspices of the Empress-Queen, in whose service he is at present a Lieutenant-Colonel, and Commander of the ship *Theresa*, he has nothing to apprehend from them; on the contrary it is the English who have everything to fear from a man of his great abilities, and who has it in his power to hurt them in India.   His wife is at my house, of which the English are very jealous, and wait to see the decided part he will take for one or two months to come, and of which I shall inform you.

Your last letter makes me very uneasy by the vague news which you tell me.   Everything here, you say, is in confusion, you will soon know the result.   Does Ragabah triumph thro' the means of the English, as is reported here by that nation?   If so, we must give it up, and such a change must involve you in a state of embarrassment.   Pray make me easy on this point. . . ."

(7) From M. le Chevalier de St Lubin to M. Anquetil de Briancourt, 15th October 1777.

"I now give you the news I had promised you, and you will say it is pretty good work for a dead man, if my friends still make me pass for one.

The army commanded by Aripundet, composed of 60,000 horse and 20 thousand foot will continue its operations against Hyder Aly. It has two objects in view, the one to make him pay the Chout,[1] the other to prevent his meddling in Ragobah's affairs. . . . In eleven days they are to be in action.

Another army commanded by Brimrow, composed of 40,000 horsemen and 10,000 foot soldiers, with a considerable train of artillery, march straight into Guzurat, where it is to be joined near Brodera[2] by Passe Sing's forces to go and fight Govinrow as far as Amadabad.[3]   He is another friend of Ragobah's, put in play by those who dare do nothing themselves.

Another army commanded by Ramsandy Gonef, composed of 20,000 men, are gone to be on the watch in the Concan from Bombay to Surat.

---

[1] The tribute levied by the Mahrattas, like the Danegeld, for abstention from ravage.   It was equivalent to one-fourth of the revenue of the country thus laid under contribution.

[2] Baroda.   [3] Ahmadabad.

At the same time the Maratta fleet will cruize along the whole of the coast between these two places.

You now see one of the best concerted plans for a campaign that has been seen for a long while. Judge whether the fever will not become epidemic from Bombay to Baroche.[1] These are the outlines of the picture of 1777 which I gave you in my last.

You are very fortunate, Sir, in having it in your power to serve such a man as Mr Bolts, whose heart and head do honour to human nature. He has defended its cause against tyranny with that vigour which can alone proceed from virtue. His work is one of the chief ornaments of my library. I carried it to the Minister as soon as it made its appearance. Its similarity with my writings on the same subject struck him so forcibly, that if mine had not been anterior, I might have been taxed with either collusion or plagiarism. If he remains only three years longer in India, he will see all his predictions fulfilled. As to his commerce, it is sufficient that the Empress-Queen has entrusted one of her ships to him, for every Frenchman to favour it. Therefore, Sir, let you and I act in concert to procure M. de Sartine the satisfaction of paying his court to the Queen. The following is the plan which my regard for that Minister suggests to me. . . .

If the Nabob of Surat, who is always tormented by apprehensions and by the English, should refuse your demands in favour of the ship *Theresa*, the resource of the Marattas is open to him; but not to affect your personal interest, I would take the following course. Pandaba Lacre shall buy his cargo which is in your hands at Surat. Your duties will be paid there, and the ship shall go from thence to unlade at Chaoul. By this expedient I shall serve you all. I wish for nothing but glory. Pandaba is this instant set off for Surat to know the nature, quality, quantity, and price of the goods. . . ."

(8) From M. Anquetil de Briancourt to M. de St Lubin, 20th October 1777. He writes recommending a young Frenchman of good birth, M. Charlevalli,[2] Chevalier d'Anaclet, for employment in fortification. Mr Shaw, one of the Council at Bombay, had met him at Cairo and given him letters of recommendation to Ragobah and to Mr Hornby. " I have made

[1] Broach.
[2] From a letter addressed by the Surat Council to the Bombay Government, it appears this gentleman subsequently turned his professional knowledge to account by making a sketch of the plan of Surat Castle. His papers fell into the hands of the English in November 1778.

him understand," he continues, "that Ragobah's power was no more."

(9) From the same to the same, 25th October 1777.

"Mr Bolts now takes his departure for Poonah. He will deliver you these few lines together with the letter I gave him for you the 17th of last month, to the contents of which I must refer you. I think you will be much pleased to meet this amiable man who possess so good an understanding and so much knowledge. His intention is to form a settlement in India in the name of the Empress-Queen. The English thwart him as much as they can, and look upon him as one of their greatest enemies. They laugh from the teeth outwards at his projects, as they do at yours, but I trust they will not laugh always. Mr Bolts seems to have fixed on Goga to form his residence. If my views had been followed in the beginning, we should have had a Settlement there now; but that is the case with us Frenchmen, we are the first to conceive plans and the last to execute them. Pray recall to mind what I have formerly told you on this head. You even answered me that you had been busied in it. M. Bolts will certainly have occasion for your assistance at the Court of Poonah; I am persuaded it will be a pleasure to you to oblige him, and that you will on your part do for him more effectually what I have endeavoured to do for him here. Send me a pattamar to advise me of his arrival at Poonah. I have flattered him with an account of the good reception he would meet with from you; I am sure I shall not be mistaken and that you will be pleased with my sending him to you. M. Paxal would also pay you his compliments, but M. Bolts comes to see you unknown to everybody except his wife and myself. I long to know what impression the interview between you and M. Bolts makes on the English."

(10) From the same to the same, 26th October 1777.

.   .   .   .

"The object of the present is to convey the whole" (*i.e.* of his correspondence) "to you, if possible, before you see M. Bolts, that you may know beforehand what you are to look for on his account, and to prepare you for his visit, to which he has certainly been disposed by the interests of his nation and his scheme for a settlement at Goga, so that I think you will not be sorry for my apprizing you of everything concerning him; I am, however, ignorant whether this letter will reach you before M. Bolts arrives. He proceeds in his vessel to Danon, where I have recommended him to one of the principal Christians in that little town, and from thence he will continue his journey to Poonah with the utmost speed and secrecy. I acquainted you, yesterday, what are his present views in going to the Court of Poonah; I think he will be able to succeed if you give him your assistance; it will be, perhaps, an additional stroke to Bombay for you. However, weigh well the loss and gain. We are beforehand with him in seeking for a French Residence at Goga; I was the first person who demanded it of the Marattas; and I do not at all doubt but you will now obtain it. If my scheme had been approved, we should now have had a flag there, and formed a good factory, which in a little time might have ruined the trade of Bombay and Surat. A ship of war might have remained there a year without any fear of the winter. Your negotiations at Poonah and my secret operations here might, during that time, effect this great work. M. Bellecombes would certainly enter into it very willingly, that the *Brilliant* might winter at Goga as she had done at Trincomalee, it is the same expense to the nation, but the benefit arising from it is very different and entirely to our advantage. The Minister cannot but approve so excellent a manœuvre. There is yet time for it, and I am quite ready to devote myself to what the good of the nation may require of me; but as to what concerns M. Bolts, are there no means of uniting our two nations in this projected new Settlement? Perhaps the hour of our possession is remote, perhaps it is near at hand. M. Bolts's is certain and nearly approaching, if he obtains the permission for it which he goes to solicit at Poonah in the name of the Empress-Queen. His ship is already there, and his people are situated on shore on the best ground of Goga. It is for you to determine, Sir, now how far you may employ your influence with the Marratta Ministry in favour of M. Bolts's negotiations. and what advantage to France you can derive from thence against the common enemy. Pray communicate to me your ideas and the resolutions you may have taken on this head, in order that I may act in conformity thereto. I should not omit to acquaint you that M. Bolts is very communicative of all he knows against the English and on indifferent subjects, but very reserved on what concerns his operations and proceedings; that the English is his native tongue, that he speaks the French, Persian, and Moor's languages very well, and that having no need for an interpreter to treat with the people of the country, it will be difficult for you to fathom him, if he should, contrary to his interest, conceal rather too much from you. Though I am persuaded he will place an entire confidence in you, at least he has told me so, I should apprize you of this in order that you may not be taken unawares in case of the contrary. He will converse with you respecting Dhaligoa where he established a residence and left a writer and some soldiers. He will tell you of the mortifications he experienced at S'urat, and perhaps of the good offices I have endeavoured to render him ; of his intentions respecting Goga and any other places he may find, and that in fine two ships of the same destination and similar to his will not fail to appear soon in India. This and my former letters will supply what he may not inform you of, so that you will be thus sufficiently instructed to know in what manner you should act, whether he imparts his plan to you, or whether he conceals the extent of it from you. It is said here that Goga depends on Amdabat,[1] which accounts for it to Poonah. If it be so, perhaps a double negotiation may be necessary, if you treat for this place on behalf of our nation ; but I am assured on the other hand that the Court of Poonah can itself finish the affair without any further appeal. . . .

M. Picot tells me that ships of war are returned as last year to the coast ; they will undoubtedly go up as high as Choul and Surat, and perhaps to Goga, if M. Bellecombe has taken into consideration what I represented to him on the subject. Letters from England in June and the beginning of July uniformly speak of peace between the French and the English ; for the rest, M. Bolts will tell you all the news of Europe."

Postscript to the letter of the 26th, 29th October 1777.

"The English are making an attempt on Guzurat. They pretend they are going to chastize Futly Sing and seize Brodera,[2] but they have just met with a check . . . at a large town called Mai Canta Devane.[3] . . . This first check they met with would have made them abandon the enterprize, if Governarrow,[4] who is at or very near Amdabat,[5] would have united his forces with his brother Futly Sing's. Are there no means, Sir, of acting secretly at Poonah to effect this union ? "

(11) From Mr William Bolts to M. de Boicervoise, French Deputy-Consul at Surat, dated Goga the 28th October 1777.

"This serves to put into your hands the dispatches with which you are pleased to charge yourself, and which I must beg you to

---

[1] Ahmadabad.　　　　　　　　　　　　[2] Baroda.
[3] Mahi Kantha, at the foot of the Aravalli Hills, to the north of Ahmadabad.
[4] Govind Rao.　　　　　　　　　　　　[5] Ahmadabad.

transmit to the Minister of Her Majesty the Empress-Queen, in case you have not an opportunity of presenting them in person at Vienna. From the good accounts which M. Anquetil has given me of you, and from the zeal which I have observed in you for the interests of my expedition, I have recommended you to Prince Kaunitz,[1] to secure a good place for you in our new establishments, in case that should suit you. It is for this reason, and because you can tell the Minister, as having been an eye-witness, everything that has passed at Surat respecting my ship, that I am charmed with the opportunity you have of making yourself known at Vienna. If I had time, I should give you other letters, particularly to my friends M. de Raab and M. d'Herbert. If you go to Vienna, you will be acquainted with them, and make my compliments to them, for at present I have but just time to wish you a prosperous voyage, which I do with assurances that I am with the most perfect consideration, Sir, your most obedient and most humble servant,   WM. BOLTS."

(12) From M. Anquetil de Briancourt to M. Belle-combes, French Governor-General at Pondicherry, 12th November 1777.

"The Nabob yesterday caused to be delivered to me the answer to your letter, which I had so often demanded of him. I transmit it to you enclosed. The English at Bombay have not yet made me satisfaction for the stairs. . . . They however promise me that satisfaction. . . . This incident will not, however, hinder the reception of French vessels here, even ships of war. I have announced them to Mr Boddam, with whom I am constantly on very good terms. . . .
. . . The English assure us that in the month of July there was no war declared between France and England. . . .
You are not surely ignorant, Sir, of what passes at Poonah, and that it is just decided that the campaign shall be opened with three different armies. . . . This is the plan which M. de St Lubin has lately imparted to me; it is well concerted, and must produce a great effect if well executed.
The Imperial ship the *Theresa*, commanded by Mr Bolts, has been arrived in this Road these two months. He had run ashore at Daligoa, as you must certainly have heard, Sir, but got the ship off. Mr Bolts, formerly second at Benares, at present Lieutenant-Colonel in the Empress-Queen's service, and banished by the English for having opened the eyes of the British Ministry on the oppressions of Bengal, could land nowhere at Surat but at my house, where I

---

[1] Prince Wenceslaus Anton von Kaunitz, Austrian Ambassador at Paris from 1748 to 1753, when he returned to Vienna and became Chancellor of State.

entertained him as well as I could, together with his wife who was with him. The Nabob, at the instigation of the English, refused him any succour, and permission to land his merchandize, except on paying twenty per cent. I furnished him with as many provisions as I possibly could, and received all his sick into my garden. The Empress-Queen, who in the warmest manner patronizes Mr Bolts and his new commercial establishment, will not surely be pleased with the reception the English have given him here. For my own part, notwithstanding my negotiations with the Nabob, I have been able to afford him and his family nothing more than barely hospitable entertainment. This makes me still more cautious in my behaviour and produces me many enemies, whose threats however have little effect on me, and for which I shall be still less inclined to alter my conduct. Mr Bolts, fearing the Coup de vent de la Saint François,[1] has sheltered his vessel at Goga, where she yet remains.

Foreigners, Sir, profit by our discoveries. M. Le Roy's soundings which I had sent there served for Mr Bolts. What should hinder one of our ships of war wintering there this year, if the plan of operations should require it? Mr Bolts designs to sell his cargo at Goga. He has left his wife with me, who is in good health, and his sick officers. He is just gone on a little vessel which he bought at Danon near Daman, and must have gone from thence by land to Poonah, where I believe him to be now arrived. He is gone to solicit of the Maratta Ministry a residence at Goga, and the right of a flag, in the name of the Empress-Queen. As he had communicated his schemes to me, I gave information of all to M. de St Lubin, who will without doubt do everything for the best, without derogating from our rights of precedence at Goga, of which I made a demand upwards of two years ago. The English are much confounded at Mr Bolts's plan, and dread the consequences. Two other Imperial ships, which left Europe with the same object in view, should shortly appear in these seas. As soon as I know the result of the interview between M. de Lubin and Mr Bolts, and the end of the negotiations with the Maratta Court as to the Imperial ship, I will impart the same to you immediately.

I am so weak, Sir, that it is with infinite pains I write this letter. . . .

My Secretary is also sick. . . .

An Englishman told me yesterday, Sir, that the last advices from London say that the English and French squadrons were at sea, but that it was not known what route either of them had taken, whither they were going, or whether they were to come to an engagement in case of meeting. A small vessel has been lately dispatched from

---

[1] See note, page 154.

L

Bombay for Suez, to carry to London the news of Mr [1] Clavering's death in Bengal. The English are making great preparations at Bombay, in order, as they say, to conduct Ragobah to Poonah. Under this false pretence they make ready for a sudden visit from the French, if by chance they should come there; but the English have hardly any people at Bombay, and still fewer at Surat.

Never was any circumstance so favourable to the French, in case of a revolution. The English have just sent from hence from six to seven hundred men towards Baroche, with a view, as they say, to bring a Cooley to reason, who refuses to make good his payment. They have met with a check, but say they have absolutely conquered him. This black detachment must return, for Surat is not otherwise guarded."

(13) From M. Anquetil de Briancourt to M. de St Lubin, 24th November 1777.

"I take the opportunity of the pattamar which Mrs Bolts sends to her husband, to whom I have not time to write, and whom I beg you will embrace on our behalf, to acquaint you speedily of a mistake I made, which will not affect you, but which may be prejudicial to me. It is this" (a mistake regarding a Bill of Exchange).

(14) From M. de St Lubin to M. Anquetil de Briancourt, 25th November 1777.

"Mr Bolts arrived here the 18th of this month, and after your recommendation you may easily imagine the reception he met with. I immediately went to the Prime Minister Nana Fernies, to acquaint him of the affair. I requested him to receive my guest as an officer belonging to a Queen who was the mother of ours, a Power who formed a common cause with us, and I asked for a favourable hearing of the propositions he had to make, if they had nothing in them contrary to the Maratta and French interests. In consequence of this he had his audience yesterday afternoon, and returned from it much pleased. In his conversation with Nana he perceived the English had already injured him by representing him as a fugitive from the Company, an adventurer, etc. He defended himself successfully against these odious imputations and the Minister appeared to be satisfied with his apology. In reply to

---

[1] General Sir John Clavering, whose coarse violence was united with the refined malignity of Francis in the Supreme Council at Calcutta in opposition to Hastings. The third of the trio, Colonel Monson, had died a year previously.

what Mr Bolts alledged in not having brought any presents, because he had not permission to unlade anything at Danon, he said it was sufficient that he brought a letter from his Sovereign, whose union with the King of France he was acquainted with. You must allow, Sir, this may be termed a well turned compliment and highly flattering to the Family Compact,[1] the tenor of which I had explained to this Minister, who conversed with Mr Bolts on the subject with great attention.[2]

Mr Bolts cannot see the King, because his mourning keeps him from all affairs of state for a year. As to his business, Nana has sent him to Krickenrow, the Counsellor of State, who, as you know, reports French affairs to the Council. It is a very delicate attention on the part of Nana towards France, and I owe him my acknowledgments for it. M. Bolts, on his arrival, replied to the proposition I made to him to make use of the channel of Krickenrow to treat on his affairs, that he did not need anybody, as he would do everything by himself and his Secretary. Thus you may make yourself perfectly easy as to your speculations. I have them at heart for two reasons, because they belong to you, and because they will belong to us. As to the rest, I shall exert my endeavours to render my guest's life agreeable. As he showed a desire of mortifying the English by an air of parade, at his visit to Nana, I gave him my elephant, my guards, my horses, all my train except my colours. He lodges with me, and I have told him I shall consider the least expense he may be at during his stay here, even for his servants, as a breach of hospitality. His palanquin bearers having quitted him to return to Danon, I have hired ten more at my own expense for his use. I have done the same thing respecting the peons, mausalgies,[3] camaties,[4] etc., and my soldiers mount guard at his apartments in the same manner as at mine. I have brought the principal merchants to him, in order to instruct him in the trade. My Divan having told me that he was uneasy for his bills of exchange upon Bombay, I offered him my purse for any money he might have occasion for. In fine I study continually to seek for

---

[1] The Pacte de Famille, the treaty uniting the French and Spanish Bourbons.

[2] In the letter from Bengal to the Directors, in the Secret Department, of the 2nd of January 1778, signed by Hastings, Francis, and Barwell, mention is made of advices from the Resident at Poona, reporting that Mr Bolts on his arrival took up his residence with the Chevalier de St Lubin, through whose influence he was well received at the Durbar, and presented with a nuzzer of Rs. 500, a compliment paid only to persons publicly deputed to the Mahratta Court.

[3] Mashalchis, torch-bearers.

'Kamathi, common labourer, also petty retail dealer; here probably employed as "water-carrier."

what may give him pleasure, and prevent not only his demands [1] but even his wishes. I think he will leave me very well satisfied, and I thank you for having afforded me this opportunity of shewing you the power your recommendation will always have over me; and must desire you will consider it as absolute.

I received from M. Bolts the handsome arms which you committed to his charge for me; I accept with gratitude this present, magnificent as it is; but when I think of the engagement formed in my last letter, I must appear like a lazy sort of a gentleman, a lawyer without a cause, for ladies such as yours [2] can have no enemies. I request you to lay my respectful homage at their feet."

(15) From M. Anquetil de Briancourt to M. de Sartines, Minister at Paris, 24th November 1777.

. . . .

"M. Boicervoise . . . will give you every explanation you can desire respecting the commercial transactions of the French Settlement at Surat . . . he will represent to you the critical situation in which I find myself, as well through want of money, as through the necessity of providing it, and the impossibility of finding any here. He has himself advanced for the support of this Settlement the sum of rupees 5448, and the sale of effects which belonged to me having produced Rs. 25,009, annas 14, I advanced that sum for the same object, as you will see by my books. . . .

These present dispatches, Sir, contain also the duplicates and triplicates of my letters of the 2nd, 3rd, and 12th April last, and copy of three letters written to foreigners; the first to the Governor-General of Goa, to demand a residence at Daman, the second to the English Council of Surat, and the third to the English Council of Bombay. The two last relate to my stairs which the English caused to be pulled down by the Nabob, and of which I gave you an account at the time. They are much incensed against me respecting the stairs, as since they have been in possession of the Fort, I have been the only one who dared to tell them the truth boldly and openly. . . . I transmit you copy of a letter from the English Company to their Settlement in Bengal. This letter explains the cause of all the affronts we receive in India from the people of the country and the conduct which the servants of the Company pursue respecting us. . . . If we cannot make reprisals, we should not, in case of an affront, lay the blame upon the people of the country, who groan under the yoke. The text

---

[1] Probably the translation should have been "anticipate . . . his requests."

[2] M. Anquetil had a large family.

of the English letter is too clear to be mistaken in this respect, and it is only for having explained it, and having undeceived the public on this occasion, that the English at Surat are so much incensed against me. But supported by your protection, Sir, and acting in all things for the good of the nation, I fear the English in nothing, and am prepared for every event. I must request that you will communicate to the English Ambassador the extract of a letter from that Company, who are, notwithstanding the most pacific disposition on our part, the origin of all disorders and the source of all quarrels in India. The order will be revoked without doubt, since we are at peace, and our privileges will be no more infringed. Thence follows, Sir, by the most natural consequences, the re-establishment of the French flag at Surat. The rights of the nation, its honour, and its credit require it to be so, and I only wait your orders to hoist the flag in the French garden, the place of its first existence.

In order that you may have no information wanting, Sir, on what concerns the political affairs of the English at Bombay and Surat, regarding Ragonath Row or Ragobah, who is constantly at Bombay, waiting till the English be in force to replace him on the throne of Poonah ; and that you may also be acquainted with everything respecting the Maratta Court, and what we may expect from it, I send you my correspondence with M. le Chevalier de St Lubin ; it commences from the instant when I knew of his arrival by your order at Poonah. You will see what an effect his mission of Ambassador and Minister from France had on the English, and how they fear him ; you will likewise see the obstacles they raise to the success of the operations of the ship *Maria Theresa* belonging to the Empress-Queen. As I have entered into this subject at large with M. de St Lubin, it would be merely repetition to trouble you farther upon it.

I shall only add, that the English bear me much ill will for the assistance I afforded to the ship, the Commander of which came to seek an establishment in India in the name of the Empress-Queen ; and that you must surely approve of the favourable reception I have given here to one under the protection of that august Princess. In my next I shall give you an account of Mr Bolts's further negotiations, and of the operations of this Imperial ship, for the success of which M. de St Lubin and myself have united our zeal, without however derogating from the rights and prerogatives of our own nation.

I have closed my correspondence with M. de St Lubin with an extract of his last letter, the communication of which will, I think, give you pleasure, and I also send you copy of my letter to M. de Bellecombes, in order that you may be able to sum up what respects that part of India which is at present most agitated.

The last news from Bengal says that Mr Hastings will resign the government of that Presidency to Mr Barwell, who is at present second, by the death of Messrs Clavering and Monson, as soon as Mr Wheler the Counsellor shall arrive from Europe."

After recording the deposition, imprisonment, and death of Lord Pigot, and the arrest of all the leading actors in the Madras tragedy, he continues: "From Bombay there is nothing absolutely interesting. Ragonath Row is constantly kept there by the English as a mere phantom, and held forth as a scarecrow to the Minister of Poonah, where M. de St Lubin takes care effectually to destroy the illusion. M. Carnac, Colonel and an old Commander in the Bengal forces, who is come to supply Mr Hornby's place, forms a little division in the Council, because Mr Hornby seems disposed, in order to thwart him, always to keep the reins of Government.

My correspondence with M. de St Lubin will inform you of all the political affairs of this coast. I must repeat my instances, Sir, that you will take into consideration what concerns this Settlement relative to the French flag, and to continue to me your protection.

I have not yet been favoured with the receipt of any of your orders. Enclosed are two letters from M. de St Lubin."

(16) From M. Anquetil de Briancourt to M. de St Lubin, 1st December 1777.

.   .   .   .

"I hear nothing further of M. Bolts. Pray, Sir, inform me how you are with him. Does he succeed in his negotiations with the Court of Poonah? Will he have Goga, on which he so entirely depends? I am however very easy in that respect because you are there, otherwise I should absolutely fear for our precedence, which though of right, is notwithstanding capable of being made to agree with the pretensions or demands of M. Bolts; but I depend on you entirely in the affair, and must beg you will give me some few satisfactory particulars of his proceedings. . . ."

(17) From the same to the same, 6th December 1777.

.   .   .   .

"I have this instant, Sir, received your letter of the 25th of last month. . . . I give you a thousand thanks for your obliging attention to M. Bolts, and to the recommendation I gave him to secure the good reception you have given him. I expected no less from your friendship for me and from your penetration in discovering the personal merit of M. Bolts. It is a very fortunate circumstance for him to have met you at Poonah; he would otherwise have been much embarrassed to negotiate at the Court, especially on account of the King's mourning, and the delays he must have submitted to but for your mediation, which will undoubtedly shorten his work. I have read your letter a second time, I am so charmed with it in every respect. The generosity which reigns in it throughout to M. Bolts as your guest, the preparation you have made for his visit, the measures you take not to expose our interests while you labour to forward the views of the Empress-Queen at the Maratta Court, the success of M. Bolts's first audience, part of his (? 'your') suite being put in employ, dresses, etc., all this gives me the most sensible pleasure. . . . *P.S.*—I doubted much whether M. Bolts would treat entirely by himself with the Minister; he had taken with him all his people for the purpose, but he reckoned without his host. He has left on board his ship upwards of 15 thousand musquets, they say, with cannon and ammunition in proportion. He will undoubtedly have trusted to you to dispose of them at Poonah. Apropos of arms, are the three bodies of Maratta troops in the field?"

(18) From M. de St Lubin to M. Anquetil de Briancourt, 8th December 1777.

"M. Bolts after having met with the reception from Nana which I mentioned to you in my dispatches of the 25th November, had an audience of Sataran Bapore. He has tried every manœuvre for these fifteen days past to treat in the matter himself; but at last having received a positive answer from Government that he could not do better than employ the mediation of the Minister from France, he resolved to desire I would charge myself with his negotiation. He had his audience of leave [1] of the Minister yesterday. To-day he sets out for Bombay from whence he will return to Surat. I charged him with the French translation of his work against the Company for you, and a housing for your amiable Amazon's [2] horse etc."

(19) From the same to the same, 13th December 1777.

.   .   .   .

"If the questions you ask me respecting M. Bolts in your letters of the 1st and 6th December still remained questions with you,

---

[1] It should be "farewell audience."
[2] Apparently one of M. Anquetil's daughters; unless Mrs Bolts is meant.

after reading my dispatches of the 8th, I should believe you have not perfectly understood me. You have every reason to be satisfied. He has been refer'd to me, and I am, as I have told you, charged with managing his business. He set off for Bombay the 9th.

I am much hurt at finding you are so little visited by our ships. . . .

I had entertained hopes of rectifying this ill-luck a little, by proposing to you, for M. Bolts, the settlement offered by Pandeba Lacre of buying his cargo in your hands at Surat, paying you the duties. That was the sense of my letter of the 15th October; but when at his arrival here I showed him that letter in my book, so far from finding him disposed towards you as I expected, he talked of nothing but selling at Goga, and of the steps he had taken with the Chief of that place as to his commerce. I suffered him to proceed, till after the most vigorous efforts he found out that his arrangements amounted to nothing at all. If on his return to Surat he appears to be more tractable, you can write me upon it, and I will settle the matter immediately. I find your words he reckoned without his host not only strictly true, but perhaps the proverb was never better applied. . . .

The three armies are in motion. . . . The English . . . kindle the fire of this war to destroy the two powers" (Haidar Ali and the Mahrattas) "by means of each other, and then to rise upon the double ruin. I labour very hard to extinguish the flame; but Hyder must pay, and the quantum is the point on which both parties must hearken to reason. I shall effect it."

(20) From the same to the same, 17th December 1777.

.   .   .   .

" I am obliged to you for what you tell me of M. Bolts's transactions at Poonah, and I felicitate myself on having apprized you of every thing which I think may have been of service to you. Pray do me the favour of letting me know soon, how far your mediation has contributed (and which it must have done without doubt) to the success of his affairs. I shall learn nothing from him, because he is too reserved to those who wish him well, and who are in a situation to serve him, not for their interest but for his own. I have besides another point of delicacy. I would not appear to sell him hospitality, and that is the opinion he might form of me, were I to show myself too curious.

I am under a thousand obligations to you for M. Bolts's work in French; it will be here in ten or twelve days, and I shall acknowledge the receipt of it. I hear no talk of the three armies; pray acquaint me whether the Marattas are still of the same mind. . . .

A Frenchman at Bohonajore near Goga, and in the service of the Rajah of that place, writes me word that the said Rajah is sold to the English, and that the merchants are so far intimidated by the Nabob of Surat's menaces, that he believes M. Bolts will be able to do nothing on that side. . . .

There is nothing further said here about any French ships. . . . Do you expect any ships at Chaoul? . . . Do not forget Goga. Damans will have its day beyond a doubt. The obstinate silence of the Minister does not slacken my zeal for the nation, but vexes me very much. . . ."

(21) From the same to the same, 27th December 1777.

. . . .

" As to myself, don't be uneasy about me; for seventeen years that I have lived at Surat, I have been accustomed to live by my shifts; it is true the service suffers from it; for if I had money to subsist myself and provide for the Settlement, there would not perhaps, without flattering myself, be a more extensive and interesting correspondence in India than mine. I have neither a taste for play, the table, or parties of pleasure. I love a small society composed partly of ourselves and partly of strangers, and above all my own closet; but as I am anxious to see the French nation make as great a figure in India as foreigners, this cannot be done without money, and that ruins me. If . . . the means of providing this Settlement were sent me . . . I should have more ability to exert for the service . . . all my correspondence is then in motion. I know what passes among the Marattas, at Bombay, in the Red Sea, the Persian Gulph, at Delhi, and even in Bengal, without speaking of the Malabar and Choromandel. Coasts and China; my closet . . . becomes my only delight . . . where . . . all the political and commercial news of the above places meet. . . . But when one must be continually contriving how to make the pot boil, which by the bye is a very material object, whatever Philosophy may say, it enervates the imagination and makes all correspondence lanquid. . . .

. . . An Empty stomach has no ears. . . . I have requested M. de Sartines to honour me with his protection in some other post, or to assure to me some emoluments in this. . . . I have further requested him to allow the nation to enjoy the privilege it has from the Nabob of hoisting a flag. I have sent him all the papers that prove that right. Besides this right is an appendage to the station of Consul from France, wherever he may happen to reside ; but there are much stronger reasons for it at Surat where this privilege subsists, and where it is necessary that the French flag should be hoisted, as well for the honour of the nation as for its credit among the people of the country. . . .

I shall only add that M. Bolts is not yet arrived at Bombay, that as soon as he returns here I shall employ all my rhetorick to induce him to adopt the plan you have proposed to him for his cargo. If he accepts it, which I doubt, I shall receive at least 15,000 rupees in duties for the King. Good Heaven! How well the affairs of the closet would go on for about 12 or 15 months ! . . ."

Postscript to the above letter, dated 30th December 1777.

.   .   .   .

"Hyder Ali Khan is very successful in his enterprizes. . . . By the first mission to M. Contannan and that at present entrusted to M. Duplessix you will judge of the terms we are on with that Conqueror.

. . . The English troops sent from Surat into the neighbourhood of Baroche are on their return. . . . They give out that they have brought two Coolie Chiefs to reason who refused to pay the revenue of their jaghires. I forgot to thank you, Sir, for your good wishes towards the Settlement of Surat, which I see by the commercial scheme you have engaged for M. Bolts to adopt. I think he will do nothing in it, and so much the worse for him and for me respecting the duties. I am moreover much obliged to you, and the Minister cannot but be mighty pleased with the address with which you have turned into your own hands M. Bolts's negotiations with the Court of Poonah, and especially his pretensions respecting Goga. . . ."

(22) From M. Anquetil de Briancourt to M. de Sartines, 30th December 1777.

"I had the honour of writing you on the 24th of last month, aud sending M. Boicervoise, Chief Deputy of this Settlement, charged with my dispatches for you. . . .

My annexed correspondence with M. de St Lubin contains new extracts of letters dated since M. Boicervoise's departure.

As I flatter myself that you would wish to read this last part of my correspondence . . . I shall not revert to the news of the Malabar Coast, contained in the last letters, neither to the operations of M. Bolts here and at Goga, or his fruitless negotiations at Poonah, which will only assume a favourable aspect in proportion to M. de St Lubin's labours in that behalf. . . ."

(23) From M. Perier de Salvert, on board the King's ship *le Curzieux* at Bombay, to M. Anquetil de Briancourt.

"Being sent by M. de Bellecombes to the Malabar Coast to deposit some stores at Myhie,[1] . . . I thought it my duty to take an account of the reports which have been spread of an alliance concluded with the Marattas by M. de St Lubin. I have in consequence come to an anchor at Chaoul, and have learnt that M. de St Lubin was arrived at Poonah . . . with a suite composed of sailors dressed as guards and shipboys as pages ; that he had there assumed the character of Minister from the Court of France, making his followers qualify him with the title of My Lord, and no longer allowing of letters from the Captain of the *Sartine*, but requiring memorials and petitions. That after having promised the said Captain that his cargo should be sold free of duty, he had caused the Marattas to demand a large sum for anchorage and other duties ; that the Marattas not being willing to pay for the goods but at a low price, and the season advancing, M. Coronat found himself obliged to borrow about Rs. 400,000 of a Bramin at 8 per cent. for 6 months, in order to complete the ship for the China voyage, and that the cargo from Europe remained with M. Coronat in the hands of the Marattas as security for the sum borrowed.

That M. de St Lubin on the hopes given to the Marattas of a body of 600 Europeans, and upon the assurance that he acted in concert with M. de Bellecombes, has signed a conditional treaty with them. That for some time he preserved the confidence of the Maratta Durbar, which had granted him 400 rupees a month allowance and a guard for his camp . . ., but that the oppression he has exercised towards all the Europeans in his suite, two of whom put themselves under the protection of the English, has begun to alienate the minds of the Marattas.

That the English, uneasy to the last degree, immediately on the receipt of this intelligence, sent a Counsellor of Bombay to Poonah, with 200 sepoys commanded by European officers, under pretence of treating on the affairs of Ragoba, the sovereign dethroned by the Marattas and protected by the English, who afford him an asylum at Bombay.

That these Englishmen, now at Poona, endeavour to convince the Marattas that it is trusting to a Chimera, to depend on the promises of M. de St Lubin, not acknowledged by the Governor-General of Pondicherry, and who is personally known to have formerly abused the confidence of the English, the French, and Hyder Ally Khan.

---

[1] Mahé.

That the latter beholds with astonishment a negotiation entered upon in the name of France with his enemies, without his having been apprized of it, and at the moment when he shows us the greatest regard. . . .

Though I may have been deceived in some particulars, be assured I have spared nothing to get at the truth. If I had only heard the stories of men inflamed against M. de St Lubin, I should not have finished so soon; but I have related to you what agrees with the report of impartial persons, and what I conceived besides to be particularly interesting to Government.

The English have not failed to seize this occasion to espouse Ragoba's quarrel against the Marattas; but they have received the most positive orders from Europe, not to engage in any war in India, at a time when no assistance either of men or ships could be given from home."

.   .   .   .

In the month of May 1779 M. de St Lubin, who had left Poona for Damaun, then, as now, Portuguese territory, hatched a plot for bringing down a body of Mahratta troops to lay the city and district of Surat under contribution.

A few weeks later this design was changed into a plan for seizing on the city of Surat and plundering it.

The French consul, M. Anquetil de Briancourt, who had been left at Surat on parole after the seizure of the French factory there and the deportation of the other French residents, was an accomplice.

The plot was disclosed by a French prisoner, Le Père Gilbert, to the Governor of Bombay. A few months later General Goddard discovered that the Dutch consul at Surat, M. Vandergraft, was also intriguing with the Mahrattas for the destruction of the English power in Surat, although there was an alliance subsisting at that time between Great Britain and the States-General.

The Chevalier de St Lubin defied the efforts of the English Government to dislodge him from Poona for a considerable period. He commanded the Mahratta artillery on the occasion of the disastrous Bombay expedition of January 1779, which ended in the humiliating convention of Wargaon. In September 1779 a spirited attempt was made by a Lieut. Robinson in the Red Sea to seize St Lubin and the vessel in which he was returning to France with important despatches. A sharp action was fought, but the Portuguese ship, in which St Lubin was sailing, escaped into shallow water under the guns of the fort at Mocha, and the English vessel was unable to follow.

CHAPTER III

MR BOLTS AT BOMBAY, AND THE
INTERCEPTED LETTER

IN the general letter to the Directors from the
Bombay Government, dated the 25th of January
1778, after reference to the account of Mr Bolts's
doings given in their letter of the previous November,
they remark:

"We conclude that the object of his journey to Poonah was to
obtain a settlement at Goga, and we shall be able to judge what
success he met with by his future proceedings, but no endeavours
were wanting on our part to oppose his design. It is surmised that
Mr Bolts, by making a settlement at Delagoa, means to make that
place his magazine for European commodities and from thence to
pour them into India.

A sloop named the *Leopold* purchased by him from the Dutch
at Surat arrived here the 16th November with a letter from him
dated at Goga the 31st October wherein he complained much of the
treatment he received at Surat, and put two queries to us which he
requested we would answer.

We accordingly sent him a reply by our Secretary a copy of
which and of Mr Bolts's letters we transmit for your more full consideration. Whilst Mr Bolts was at Poonah a packet addressed to
him super-scribed 'on their Imperial Majesty's Service' fell into the
hands of Mr Lewis thro' the mistake of the pattamars, who thought
it his duty to transmit it to us. The Captain of the sloop *Leopold*
who had by some means gained information of the packet being
intercepted demanded it from us in the name of their Imperial
Majesty's, and on consideration of the matter it was thought best to
give it up, but Mr Carnac desired it might be minuted that as Mr
Bolts was engaged in a scheme so destructive to the interests of the
Company, he thought every means should be made use of to defeat
it, and he was therefore of opinion that the contents of the packet
should have been inspected, as there was reason to conclude from

174

the anxiety of Mr Bolts's agent to recover it that it contained intelligence of importance.

Mr Bolts himself arrived here from Poona the 13th December when we immediately resolved not to permit of his stay here beyond a reasonable time for procuring the necessary supplies for the sloop during her voyage. He left this place on the 24th when we had determined to require him to depart, and on that day he sent in a letter and protest commenting on our reply to his former letter and protesting against us for the interception of his packet. A copy thereof is transmitted under No. 56 for your information, and we have to remark in reply to his complaint of the disrespect shown him by our answer being sent through the Secretary that however much we might be disposed to pay all possible respect to a commission from so illustrious a personage as the Empress-Queen, we could not consistently shew any distinction to Mr Bolts, who may justly be termed an apostate from the Company's service.

With regard to our replies to his queries we think they were as explicit as the nature of his queries required, and in our interference with the Nabob of Surat to obstruct his commercial views, we acted in exact conformity to your commands of the 21st of February which direct us to make use of our influence with the Country Powers to counteract his designs. Four British subjects deserted from Mr Bolts's ship and have entered into your service. Having received information from them of there being several others on board, we gave notice thereof to Sir Edward Vernon,[1] who has sent the *Cormorant* sloop of war to make enquiry into the affair. . . .

The *Cormorant* returned from Goga the 22nd instant, where eight British seamen voluntarily quitted the Austrian ship and entered on board the *Cormorant*."

Mr Bolts's letter of complaint to Governor Hornby and his Council ran as follows :

"You have sometime ago been informed of the accident which happened to the Imperial Austrian ship *Guiseppe and Teresa* under my command in the Bay of Delagoa. A subsequent transaction there obliges me now to lay my complaints before you on behalf of their Imperial Majesties against John Cahill, Captain of a ketch from your Presidency, the whole relation of which is briefly as follows :

On the 3rd day of May 1777 I took formal possession of a certain district of land in the country called Tembe on the Western side of

[1] A distant connection of the better-known Admiral Edward Vernon. Sir Edward was knighted in 1773 and appointed Commander-in-Chief in the East Indies in 1776.

the river Mafoomo in the before mentioned Bay from the Rajah Mohaar Capell,[1] who by a deed of sale and by a treaty solemnly executed the same day gave up the propriety and sovereignty thereof together with the sovereignty of the said river to their Imperial Majesties for ever.   There were at this time in the river Mafoomo two ketches from Bombay under English colours, one commanded by Captain John Mc. Keney and the other by Captain John Cahill, the latter of whom having partly erected a hut of Cajan[2] sticks did on the 4th of May wantonly erect a flagstaff and hoist thereon an English ensign within ten yards of the Imperial flagstaff and even within the line of the guns we had planted on taking possession. Wishing to avoid every act that should bear the smallest appearance of incivility I thereupon wrote the following letter to Captain Cahill :

SIR,—By virtue of special powers from my sovereign Her Imperial Majesty the Empress-Queen of Hungary, etc. etc., I have concluded a treaty with Rajah Capell by which he gives up to Her Majesty for ever the sovereignty of this river Tembé, alias Mafoomo, together with all the land within a certain district on the Western side thereof.   I therefore hope you will not take it amiss that I request you will not in future order any colours to be hoisted on Her Majesty's territory, where none but the Imperial colours will be permitted.   In the meantime any ground you may want to build houses or banksalls[3] on for your conveniency will be very readily allowed subject to Her Majesty's sovereignty.

To this letter Captain Cahill did not think proper to give any answer.   Nevertheless I sent several other polite messages to him by my officer requesting he would take down his ensign; but the Captain still refused to comply, at one time pretending he was going to give a dinner ashore, and at last alledging he had bought the ground or some part of it himself.   Upon this I assured Captain Cahill that if he really had purchased any ground that was comprehended within Her Imperial Majesty's territory and could prove his title to it, he should be perfectly secure of his property, subject to the sovereignty of the Power to whom the district was given up agreeable to the usages and laws of nations in similar cases.   The Rajah Capell in the meantime having informed me there was no truth in Captain Cahill's assertion of any purchase I prevailed on Captain Mc. Keney to accompany my officer whom I again sent to expostulate with Captain Cahill on the impropriety of

---

[1] In a report to his owner, Captain Cahill styles him "the Coffery king (named Copell)."

[2] Dhall, a kind of pulse.   The word is probably of Malay origin.

[3] Warehouses.   The word is probably derived from the Bengali "bankasala," trade-hall.   It is preserved in the name of Bankshall Street, Calcutta.

his conduct in endeavouring to obstruct the affairs of the Imperial Court, which I informed the Captain was highly aggravated in his person as not only acting without authority from either the British Government or the East India Company, but as being a person as I was informed not authorized (according to the laws of his own country) to be even found on this side of the Cape of Good Hope. But although Captain Cahill now thought proper to desist from his pretence of having purchased any ground, still he kept his ensign flying close to the Imperial flag, till I was at last obliged to let him know that if he did not lower it I should send my own people to do it and in that case I would even pull down the few sticks he had set up towards building a hut, as I was resolved not even a hut should be erected on Her Majesty's territory by any man in obstinate defiance of Her Majesty's sovereignty while I had power to prevent it.

Captain Cahill still paying no attention to the expostulations of my officer or even of his countryman Captain Mc. Keney, I was reduced to the disagreeable necessity of executing what I had threatened and I accordingly ordered Captain Cahill's ensign to be taken down and carried aboard his vessel.

I have been thus particular in my relation of this affair to convince you, Sirs, how scrupulous I shall be on every public transaction of acting in an offensive manner to the most unauthorized subject of your Government.   At the same time I flatter myself you will be equally ready to do my sovereigns the justice of reprimanding Captain Cahill for his obstreperous conduct.

Being safely arrived in the road of Surat though much in want of assistance and refreshment particularly on account of several of my officers and crew who were dangerously ill, I applied on that occasion by a letter of the 6th September to Governor Boddam who referred me to the Nabob as the Mogul's officer, informing me that the City of Surat was the Mogul's city under his government.

Accordingly by means of Monsieur Anquetil de Briancourt, his most Christian Majesty's Consul at Surat, I made several applications to the Nabob for such assistance only as according to the constitution of the Mogul's city I knew he could not refuse.   The delicacy however of the Nabob upon those occasions was so great and productive of delays so little reconcileable to the situations of men at the point of death as obliged me to repair to this port where I and my people have been happy to find speedier relief from the humanity of the sectaries of Brimha.[1]

These transactions and the nature of certain orders which public fame informs me have been given by Your Honourable Presidency for the obstruction of the business of Her Imperial Majesty's

---

[1] Apparently he means the Brahmans.

M

subjects and ships have induced me to dispatch the present sloop solely for the purpose of authentic information from your Honours on subjects so materially interesting to the honour of the Imperial flag and the interest of their Imperial Majesties. Your answers to the following questions I shall therefore esteem as a particular favour.

1°. Whether the Imperial Austrian ships of Europe and the Imperial country ships of Asia will or will not be admitted to the rights of hospitality and trade in the British settlements of Asia on the same footing as are admitted ships of the same denominations of the French, Portugueze and other European nations?

2°. Should the Nabob or Governour of the Moguls city of Surat on any future occasion act repugnantly to the Laws of nations with respect to any vessels under my direction, whether I am to consider him as an independent Prince acting solely from his own authority or under that of the Mogul, so that any consequent act of resentment on behalf of their Imperial Majesties would not in any wise affect the British Government of Bombay or any other part of Asia or in your opinions, gentlemen, tend to interrupt the harmony subsisting between the Courts of Vienna and London? I have the honour to assure you that in the execution of the commissions with which I am entrusted I shall most studiously endeavour to avoid giving the slightest foundation for offence to any branch of the English Company's government, and I flatter myself, I shall meet with the same exemption from those prejudices arising from a jealousy of commerce which in less enlightened times have so frequently been the bane of human society."

A reply was sent to this letter through the Secretary to the Bombay Council to the effect that the President and Council could not give any decision on the Delagoa affair until they had heard Captain Cahill's version of it; that they could not "consider mere strangers in India" entitled to the same privileges as nations that had long-established chartered companies; and that, as Governors of Surat Castle and fleet by royal firman, the East India Company would certainly resent any acts offensive to the Moguls, their allies.

"The Honourable the President and Council," he added,

"have further directed me to acquaint you that circumstanced as you have been with their Honourable Employers you must be sensible you can expect no further countenance or attention from them than what the laws of hospitality indispensibly require."

To this communication Mr Bolts replied in his very best epistolary style, which had by this time risen even to the embellishment of Latin quotation :

". . . Owing to the very extraordinary interceptions of my letters which your Honour etc. and Gentlemen are well acquainted with, and which make the subject of the latter part of this address, I do not imitate your mode (unusual as I conceive in the case before us) of answering by my Secretary, as I would not wish by any example of punctilio, much less of personal disrespect, to give cause of prejudice to the affairs of my Sovereign, who, I am sorry to say, Honourable Sir and Gentlemen, from your answers will not be able to collect much information of a satisfactory nature on the subjects of my last letter.

You are pleased to inform me in one paragraph that 'you cannot consider mere strangers in India, as entitled to the same privileges and attention in your ports, as the nations who have had establishments and traded in this country for upwards of a century and a half by virtue of royal grants and phirmands.

To this I must remark that all European nations are strangers in India, and in their own respective ports while peace subsists between them are mutually entitled to that attention and freedom of intercourse which are founded on the general laws of society, where not interrupted by particular treaties. The principles on which your Honour etc. and Gentlemen herein appear to consider the Mogul's phirmands as essential to that peace and freedom of intercourse are to me perfectly unknown. . . .

I have very attentively considered the petition said to be presented to the Mogul Emperor in 1759 on behalf of the Honourable English East India Company, together with the perwanahs, husbulhookums,[1] and firmauns said to have been obtained in consequence thereof from the Mogul's Court respecting their government of the castle and fleet of Surat as those authorities have been publicly acknowledged before the most respectable tribunals of Great Britain. The Petition to the Mogul expressly prays that the Company might be invested with those offices for the purpose of protecting the inhabitants and traders of all denominations from injustice and oppression. And the orders issued in consequence recite the petition to have been granted for the express purpose of preserving

---

[1] Literally "According to Command" royal or viceregal authorisations, so-called from the initial words of the document (Wilson's Glossary).

the Bar and sea open to all ships and vessels, that the trade of all merchants and pilgrims might meet with no trouble or impediment. And they impose on the Company the strongest injunctions of 'Care, circumspection, justice, and moderation' in the execution of those offices.

According to those acknowledged documents and the immemorial established usages of the Mogul's City of Surat, the English East India Company, in the character of Governor of the Mogul's castle and fleet, cannot permit, much less themselves occasion, in the name of the Nabob, any impediments of trade by the exaction of exorbitant and unusual duties, or even by any other breaches of humanity or acts of oppression: which were the very grounds on which they themselves dispossessed the former Nabob of his Government. And although it was admitted that the English East India Company as Governor of the said castle and fleet might be at liberty to defend them when attacked, it would be merely as servants of the Mogul: but how 'they must certainly be affected' as his allies against an European nation in amity with Great Britain, for any other act of reprisals, in retaliation of a breach of the Laws of Nations on the part of the Nabob, is a point above my powers of discussion, and must be left to the decision of the courts of Vienna and St James if ever occasion should be given for it. How far their Imperial Majesties have reason to be dissatisfied with the treatment their subjects have already received on the score of trade and hospitality at Surat I leave you gentlemen to judge.

In another paragraph I am further acquainted that circumstanced 'as I have been with your employers, I must be sensible I can expect no further countenance or attention than what the laws of hospitality indispensibly require.'

Permit me to assure you in answer to this paragraph that I have perfectly obliterated from my memory all the injuries formerly received from the English East India Company. They are dead with their author,[1] and I wish never to revive the remembrance. But my present claims having no relation to any former circumstances but to that situation alone in which I have won the honour to present myself, it is solely on behalf of their Imperial Majesties that all my applications will be made, when necessary, to the representatives of the British nation in every part of Asia.

In this point of view, I 'expect no countenance,' for the very idea would be an indignity to my sovereigns; but as I shall endeavour on every occasion to pay the strictest attention to all

---

[1] Governor Verelst died in 1785, several years after this was written. Nor can the allusion be to Colonel, afterwards Brigadier-General Smith, who was living in 1782. It is therefore difficult to say who is meant by "their author," unless he means Clive, who died by his own hand in 1774.

national rights of others, I shall also expect from you, Sir and Gentlemen, the same 'attention' to those rights from which the smallest relaxation on my part or deviation on yours might possibly be highly resented by our respective sovereigns.

I come now, Sir and Gentlemen, to that subject which gives me the most lively concern, I mean the interception of my letters by William Lewis Esq.—the British Minister at the Maratta Court of Poonah, during my late residence there, by order of your Board. The accompanying affidavit sufficiently ascertains the fact, although abundance of other proof can be legally adduced if necessary. I assure you, Sir and Gentlemen, that the object of my visit to Poonah was purely of a commercial nature, in execution of a trust reposed in me by her Imperial Majesty the Empress-Queen of Hungary, etc., etc., which in no respect could tend to interrupt the peace or harmony subsisting between the British Government and the Marattas, or any other of the Indian Powers. This open infraction, therefore, of the most sacred public rights, in time of profound peace, added to the many obstructions I have already experienced, by your orders, from the Indian Governments, make me conclude that a determinate resolution has been taken per fas aut nefas to impede all intercourse between the Court of Vienna and the Princes of India, and wholly to destroy the peaceful and lawful trade of their Imperial Majesties' subjects in Asia. In this state of insecurity for transacting any business of their Majesties or their subjects, I have no other remedy left me than that of protesting, as I now most solemnly do, on behalf of my Sovereigns Their Imperial, Royal, and Apostolic Majesties against you, Gentlemen, as representatives of the British Government, for the infraction of rights which I now complain of ; and for all the detriment and loss that may accrue to the property and persons of their subjects on this side the Cape of Good Hope in consequence of any orders issued or which may be issued directly or indirectly by your Board, or by any other agents or representatives of the British Nation in Asia.

At the same time that my duty forces me to lay this public protest before your Board, permit me to assure you that I have the honour to subscribe myself with the most profound respect, Sir and Gentlemen, your most obedient and humble servant

WILLIAM BOLTS
BOMBAY   Lieut.-Col¹ in the service of
24th December 1777.   their Impl. Majesties."

The accompanying affidavit of " John Joseph Bauer, a native and heretofore inhabitant of Oedenburgh in the kingdom of Hungary, but now actually resident at the British Settlement of Bombay," declared on oath that an express messenger sent by him with a letter to his employer, Lieut.-Col. William Bolts, had been seized at Poona by, or by the orders of, the British agent there and sent down to Bombay, and that William Lewis, Esq., the English agent, had personally informed him that he had sent all Mr Bolts's letters to Bombay by order of the English East India Company, or of the President and Council of Bombay.

CHAPTER IV

MR BOLTS ON THE MALABAR COAST
AND AT CHINSURA

IN their general letter to the Directors of the 26th of April 1778 the Bombay Government report the arrival of Mr Bolts at Bombay on the *Joseph and Theresa* from Surat on the 10th of March, their refusal of his request for permission to take in salt for ballast, and his departure on the 4th of April bound, as it was believed, for Bengal.

Further information about Mr Bolts's doings appears in a correspondence between him and the Chief and Factors at Tellicherry, reported to the Directors in a letter dated the 9th of May 1778 :

"Mr William Bolts in the Austrian ship the *Joseph and Theresa* arrived at Billiapatam[1] the 21st ult. with an intention of taking in pepper there. As this proceeding of Mr Bolts is an infringement of the Honble. Company's privileges of trade granted them by the Kings of Colastria, and that he might not plead ignorance thereof, we immediately wrote him a letter, acquainting him therewith. . . .

Copy of Mr Bolts's answer and the correspondence that ensued we enclosed under No. 11, 12, 13, and as he persisted in trading, after our having informed him of the Company's privileges, we thought it unnecessary to enter into a further discussion of them, and determined to leave the whole to the judgment of our superiors.

While the Imperial ship remained at Billiapatam, there was landed from her at that place many chests of arms; after which she proceeded to Goa where she will winter. Mr Bolts and other gentlemen belonging to the above ship remain at Billiapatam."

---

[1] In the Madras Presidency on the Malabar coast north of Cannanore. He had been invited by a Portuguese adventurer named Domingos Rodriguez, formerly employed as an interpreter at the Company's factory at Tellicherry.

In his reply to the communication from Tellicherry, in which his immediate withdrawal from Biliapatam had been demanded, Mr Bolts expressed his astonishment at the claims advanced on behalf of the Company:

" I came here with the most positive and certain knowledge that, as treaties and grants are understood among nations, the said Company possessed no exclusive grants or privileges of the nature you have described that are present in force with the reigning and lawful King of Colastria."

He passed in review the former agreements between the Company and the local Country Powers from 1756 to 1765, the abandonment of the Company's forts, and the orders issued for the withdrawal of the Company's establishment at Tellicherry, and informed his correspondents that his appearance at Biliapatam was

"with the entire sanction and approbation, not only of the Nabob Hyder Ali Caun Bahader, but also of the King of Colastria himself,[1] who has declared to me, in full Durbar that he is at present under no engagements to the Company for their possessing the exclusive privilege of purchasing and exporting of pepper or any other article of commerce in his country."

He requested to be informed whether any privileges are possessed by the Company which he has omitted to notice in this letter, and calls for an explanation of his alleged infringement of the Company's rights. As to the requisition for his departure, he replied with a flat refusal:

"In honour of the colours of my August Sovereign, I am obliged to declare to you that here, or in any other part of India, I shall never pay any attention to any similar requisition, or depart from any road or harbour sooner than may suit the conveniencing of the affairs entrusted to my direction, unless compelled thereto by force of arms."

---

[1] Mr Bolts was endeavouring to obtain the consent of both potentates, Haidar Ali and the Raja of Kalastri, to the establishment of an Austrian factory at Biliapatam.

He signs himself "William Bolts, Lieut.-Colonel in the service of their Imperial Majesties."

In answer to a second demand for his withdrawal, Mr Bolts, after replying to the arguments advanced by the Chief and Factors of Tellicherry, indicated his own position in firm but temperate language:

"All I at present contend for is, that the Austrian subjects of her Imperial Majesty, and particularly the privileged Company of Traders from the Adriatic Gulf, have, in common with all other European nations now trading to the East Indies, the right of purchasing and selling in the dominions of any Asiatic Prince or Sovereign who chuses to admit them."

He went on to expose the hollowness of their pretension to the exclusive trade of the district by remarking that while he saw with his own eyes French, Dutch, Danes, Hindus, and Mussulmen freely purchasing pepper and other articles in the district, he must beg permission to dissent from the proposition that it was a right possessed exclusively by the Honourable English East India Company, and announced his intention of continuing to trade there until he received a positive prohibition from "Hyder Ali and the King of Colastria."

In a general letter from Bengal to the Directors, dated the 14th of January 1780, there is a brief mention of Mr Bolts's attempt to lands goods near Calcutta:

"Mr Bolts has been prevented landing any goods from his ships the *Joseph and Theresa* and *Kallowrath* at or near Calcutta; but we believe his merchandize was received at Chinsura and disposed of to the Dutch. Individuals at Bombay had made consignments by the ship to persons here, of which we were induced to suffer the importation. Capt. Falkner had sold a ship belonging to Merchants here to Mr Bolts at Bombay, and we have allowed a quantity of cotton equal to the owner's demands to be landed here from his vessel."

CHAPTER V

RETURN TO EUROPE: THE IMPERIAL AMBASSADOR SUPPORTS HIS COMPLAINT

AN interesting memorandum addressed to the Directors by Captain John Buncle, dated the Cape of Good Hope, 20th December 1780, narrates how he had been despatched from Bengal by the Governor-General in February 1779 to convey the French prisoners from Chandernagore to Mauritius, how his ship had been detained there by the French authorities and himself and his officers imprisoned and half starved, and how he finally escaped, thanks to the good offices of "the famous Mr William Bolts, formerly of Bengal, now a Lieutenant-Colonel in the Imperial service and a Director of the Trieste Company," who in June 1780 arrived from the Coromandel coast at Mauritius "in the *Earl of Lincoln* Indiaman now called the *Joseph and Theresa*." The old ship seems to have been in a bad way, for Mr William Bolts, having passed Mauritius at a considerable distance to the eastward,

"proving very leaky, was obliged to put in here to repair. What little repairs he did, they made him pay so dear for, that the New Company will never let any of their ships put in here, if possible to avoid it. I suspect that Mr Bolts who is said to be a clever merchant, had (with the Armenian freighters he had on board from Madras) the purchase of the cargo of the *Osterley* in view. Although he arrived too late for the outcry, I did hear he made a great stroke with the raw silk. All I know truly of the matter is, that the piece goods of the Coromandel coast were bartered for the raw silk, which was shipped on the *Joseph and Theresa*, in bills of lading as by the Armenians; and the Colonel either bought, or so negotiated matters, that a French ship was put under Imperial colours and took in some part of the *Joseph's* cargo; the remainder was coffee from Bourbon; which place the two ships in company left in September, viz., the *Joseph and Theresa* and the *Baron of Bindar* for Cape Bon Esperance and Cadix. The difficulty of manning this new purchased ship Colonel Bolts proposed to the Government the means to remedy, by giving him the English prisoners, which they consented to, with the proviso that he should take the officers also, gratis, and divide them and the men (now only 27) upon his two ships; he signing an agreement to the French Government to deliver us all up to the Consul of France upon his arrival at Leghorn; and we all signed an obligation to him, promising not to absent ourselves from his ships, . . . and to conform to the orders of him, the said Lieutenant-Colonel William Bolts, and, if required, to work our passages to Europe in our respective callings, and, upon our arrival at any port of the Empire, to surrender ourselves to the Consul of France, to be exchanged, agreeable to the manner that may be settled between the Ministers of the two Nations. What has made me so particular in the relation of this affair is, because to it we are indebted for our liberty; for I am well assured, from the great sum the Captain of the *Osterley* gave for himself, the second officer, and one servant, to pass to France, that we who remained, having no such resources, might have been obliged to have staid on that poor island all the war, had it not been for the lucky accident of the Government's being able to put some of His Most Christian Majesty's Cash in their own pockets, by sending us away, they, as we had none to give them, would never have taken any trouble.

The treatment of Mr Bolts was humane and generous, and his deportment towards us all deserves our warmest gratitude, and has drawn me into this digression. I was obliged to procure him a certificate from two doctors (which did not cost me much) that, for an illness, I could not, without endangering my life, embark for Europe."

. . . .

" A ship under Imperial colours sailed for India, and I saw them flying on a little snow that was to sail for the Nicobars, a New Settlement of the Trieste Company's, soon after us, but to what other place in India she was to proceed to, I never did learn."

A secret memorandum was addressed to the Earl of Hillsborough, who succeeded Lord Weymouth as Secretary of State for the Northern Department in 1779, by the Chairman of the East India Company, dated the 16th of November 1781, in which the formation of an establishment at Acheen, at the north-west point of Sumatra, was strongly advocated. One of the arguments adduced was that

"it is reported that Mr Bolts, sensible and active, has already made or attempted a settlement at the Nicobar Islands; and his sagacity will scarcely overlook Acheen; especially if he is supported, as we have strong ground to believe, by an European Power, who may be desirous of sharing the benefits of commerce with India."

On the 21st of November 1781 Count Belgioioso, the Minister of the Court of Vienna in London, addressed to Lord Hillsborough a vigorous remonstrance against the seizure and destruction of the Imperial Trieste Company's vessel *La Vienne* near Madras on the 27th of January 1781, coupled with a demand for reparation, also against the treatment accorded to Lieut.-Col. William Bolts and his expedition by the express orders of the Governor-General and Council. Lord Hillsborough wrote next day to the Chairman and Deputy Chairman asking for information on the matter of these complaints. On the 24th he wrote to them again, conveying a qualified assent to the measures proposed in their letter of the 16th, but requiring that full communication of all instructions issued to their servants in India in relation to the execution of those measures should be made to himself for the King's information. He added a caution to the Directors "to take special care that no offence be given to any European Power in friendship and alliance with the King in consequence of what you shall direct."

In a second letter of the same date, 24th November, Lord Hillsborough forwarded to the Chairman another memorial from Count Belgioioso containing "additional complaints of the like nature," and signified to them His Majesty's pleasure

"that you do take the same into your consideration and acquaint me for His Majesty's information with every intelligence you may already have received from India relative to the facts so repeatedly complained of, together with such information and observations as may enable me to give without delay as satisfactory an answer as possible to Count Belgioioso."

In the Directors' letter to Bengal of 1st January 1782 copies of Lord Hillsborough's letters were transmitted, as also of the representations of Count Belgioioso, and strict care is enjoined "that no cause of offence be given to any subject of His Imperial Majesty's or to the subjects of any Prince or State whatever in amity with Great Britain."

The consequence of these repeated representations was that on the 28th of November 1781 the Chairman and Deputy Chairman submitted to Lord Hillsborough a draft circular to the Company's servants in the East Indies, in which, among other important projects, the formation of a settlement at Acheen is urgently ordered, and small settlements on the Nicobar and Andaman Islands are recommended. Directions are given to procure a sufficient tract of country by direct treaty between the Governor-General and the King of Acheen, and to make the new settlement subordinate to Bengal :

"No time must be lost in treating with the King of Acheen for an exclusive settlement, even supposing we proceed no further than to fix a small number of servants there, and to hoist English colours, in order to preclude Europeans from obtaining a residence; all which . . . must be attempted with that secrecy, vigor, and prudence, which will be necessary to ensure success. In case the Emperor's flag shall have been hoisted at, or possession taken of any place in the name of His Imperial Majesty, where you may attempt to form a settlement, care must be taken that no disrespect or proceeding of yours give just cause of offence to the subjects of His Imperial Majesty. . . ."

On the 6th of December Lord Hillsborough conveyed the King's assent to the terms of the draft circular and to the execution of the various measures proposed therein.

CHAPTER VI

THE RECONSTITUTION OF THE
OSTEND COMPANY

IN a letter from Antwerp, dated the 5th September 1781, received by the Chairman of the East India Company in November 1781, is a report of the affairs of the Imperial Trieste Company :

"You will have already heard the result of the first expeditions, and that for three ships sent out, seven have returned. The chief (Bolts) having not only employed all the money the association had raised in Europe, but also having drawn very large sums from India, made them apprehensive of future consequences, and induced them to endeavour to share them among a greater number, and to solicit fresh Letters Patent to erect their establishment into an Imperial East India Company. But the late Empress, and the present Emperor, refused entering into a negotiation before the expiration of the ten years granted to the first Association. However, the Emperor, on his mother's decease assured them of all his protection, but that he would wait the return of Bolts, who had the exclusive privilege for ten years, and who, moreover, was to make a report of the state of affairs and enterprizes, begun in those countries.

Bolts returning to Leghorn while the Emperor was in Flanders, came immediately to Brussells and had several conferences with the Emperor. Finally, the day preceding the Emperor's departure from Brussells for Paris, He gave a private audience to the Association and to Mr Bolts, in which were settled as well the private account of what was to be at the Emperor's charge, as at that of the Association ; and of the new form the Association was to adopt. As Bolts had not only been put at the head of the Commerce and direction of the whole affair, with the approbation and consent of the Empress, but had also, at the same time, been commissioned by the Emperor, in particular, to make treaties of alliance and of commerce with all the Indian Potentates he should think necessary for the purports of trade or for forming settlements, having for that effect the necessary credentials; and, moreover, having before his departure had the rank of Lieutenant-Colonel granted to him by the Emperor. He made his report to the Emperor, who, in consequence thereof, took upon Himself all the debts contracted for those establishments, maintenance of the military etc., and for which the Association remained creditor, with this condition, that she took to herself all expenses made, and to be made, for perfecting them, maintaining therein at His expense a sufficient garrison; but that each ship going to said settlements should carry out a certain number of officers and soldiers, who, during the voyage, should be maintained at the expense of the Company, but their pay etc. to be defrayed by the Emperor. That, moreover, he should grant them permission to open a subscription for two thousand actions;[1] that from the middle of September (I suppose 1781) the old Association should shut up its books, and the New Company should commence its rights and prerogatives. That they should name five Directors, three of which to reside at Antwerp, and two at Leghorn and Trieste; these to be charged particularly to manage the expeditions. That every ship so fitted out in one or the other of the Emperor's ports may, at its return, come to either of His Majesty's ports to unload and to make public sales as they may think fit. That to facilitate this trade, His Imperial Majesty promises to cause to be loaden on board each ship, for his own account, to the amount of £20,000 sterling, either in ready money, or in copper, tin, etc. of Hungary, for which the Company shall not pay interest, but only reimburse the capital thirty months after the ship's return. These are the principal articles that were granted at the audience, and which His Imperial Majesty promised should be put into proper form as soon as he returned to Vienna. This has been accordingly done; for in the beginning of August they were received, and two or three days afterwards they opened the subscription, which was filled in less than twenty-four hours. Had it been for four thousand actions, it would have been equally filled. The old Association took a thousand actions, of which they ceded two hundred to Bolts, and the remainder among the old concerned. They will send this season three ships to India, three do. to China, and three at least to the whale fishery between the Cape of Good Hope and Cape Horne; probably the future sales will be made here; and that they will keep in Italy only such articles as are fit for that country. We have had one sale of teas by the *Kaunitz*, which answered very well; the superfine was bought by the English, and the remainder by the Dutch. In March or April next we shall have another sale

---

[1] Shares. An obsolete usage.

of tea, raw and wrought silk, and China ware, that came by the last ship the *Joseph Teresa.*"

This extract was forwarded by the Chairman to Lord Hillsborough.

The following summary of the history of the Imperial Company of Trieste is taken from Macpherson's "Commerce with India":

"In the year 1775 Mr William Bolts . . . went to Vienna, where he was received by the Empress Maria Theresa as one of her subjects. In order to shew his zeal for the interest of his new sovereign and her subjects, he presented a proposal for establishing a trade with Africa and the East Indies, to be carried on under her auspices, from her ports at the head of the Adriatic Sea, to which there could be no such objection made as was urged against the establishment of an East India trade to the Netherlands. That he might be the better enabled to carry his proposal into execution, he requested the Empress to let him have an assortment of metals, canon, and small arms, from the Imperial mines and manufactories, to the amount of 180,000 florins, and to allow him two years to make the payment.[1]

The Empress approved of his proposal, and on the 5th of June 1775 signed a charter, whereby she authorizes him, during the space of ten years, to carry on trade, with vessels under the Imperial flag, from her ports in the Adriatic Sea, to Persia, India, China, and Africa; to carry negro slaves from Africa and Madagascar to America; to take goods upon freight, either for the Imperial ports, or any others, for account of foreigners, whose property shall not be liable to confiscation, even if they should belong to nations at war with her; to take possession, in her name, of any territories which he may obtain from the Princes of India; and she declares, that the vessels belonging to him, or freighted by him, and the people belonging to them, shall be exempted from arrest or detention, at all times, whether at peace or at war, that she will provide him all the necessary passports, and will take care to obtain redress for him, if he is attacked or molested.

Bolts immediately assumed Charles Proli and Company, merchants in Antwerp, as partners to the extent of one third of the business. They agreed to fit out and load two ships at Leghorn and Trieste, and that Bolts should proceed to India, in order to establish factories and conduct the business, leaving the charter in the hands of his

---

[1] The succeeding Emperor made a present of this sum to Mr Bolts and his partners.

partners with authority to establish a house of India trade at Trieste.

Bolts, having bought a ship in London, the *Earl of Lincoln*, sailed in March 1776 from the Thames. When he got out to sea, he deprived the English captain of the command, appointed a new one, and sailed, under Imperial colours, into Lisbon. There his ship was stripped of all her hands by a British frigate, and a new ship's company procured, consisting of Italian seamen. After encountering several hardships at Lisbon, he proceeded to Leghorn, whence he sailed for India.

Having settled three factories on the Malabar coast, one on the Nicobar Islands, and one at Delagoa on the coast of Africa, he returned with three ships to Leghorn, where he arrived in May 1781.

The Grand Duke of Tuscany was so much pleased to see ships from India arrive in his dominions, that, in order to testify his goodwill to Mr Bolts, he gave him a charter, dated on the 29th of May 1781, for an exclusive trade between Tuscany and all the countries beyond the Cape-de-Verd islands, to be conducted in two ships under Imperial or Tuscan colours, and to continue till the expiration of the Imperial Charter. With this additional charter in his possession, and enjoying apparently the favour of two Sovereigns in Europe and some in India, Mr Bolts felt himself in a very disagreeable situation, which was owing entirely, as he represents the matter, to the treachery of his Antwerp partners. They left him, he says, unsupported, and dishonoured his India bills, neglected to send out ships according to agreement, treacherously sent a ship from L'Orient, in 1779, and one from Leghorn, to China on their own account, without allowing him his stipulated two-thirds profit; in 1779 tried to persuade Maria Theresa to grant them a new charter, in which he (Bolts) should have no share. As soon as Bolts's ships arrived at Leghorn, his many creditors rushed thither, and got the ships and cargoes arrested. His distress compelled him to enter into a new connection with his partners. At Antwerp on August 9 1781 Bolts signed a contract ceding to Messrs Proli and Co. the Imperial and Tuscan Charters, in order to raise a joint stock of 2 million florins; he renounced his claim for profits on the 2 ships sent to China, except a 2 per cent. commission on the gross sales; he assumed the property of a ship, *The Grand Duke of Tuscany*, and of her cargo, which had been seized by the French and Dutch at the Cape in April 1781.

In return Messrs Proli agreed to lend Bolts £1280, 16s. 8d. at 5 per cent. to pay off a debt contracted on the joint account, for which they took security upon his property in the trade; they agreed that he might once send two ships to China on his own account, paying his partners 6 per cent. commission on gross sales of cargoes.

N

Their agreement was confirmed by the Emperor Joseph II., Maria Theresa's son, who authorized them to raise the sum of 2 million florins, the proposed capital of the new 'Imperial Company of Trieste for the Commerce of Asia.'

Proli and Company opened subscriptions for 1 million—they valued their existing stock at 1 million florins, of which 800,000 belonged to them, and 200,000 to Bolts.

They appointed themselves Directors at Antwerp, Bolts and another at Trieste, and reserved to the Directors a commission of 2 per cent. on gross sales in Europe.

The partners met at Antwerp in September 1781 and agreed to send 6 ships for China and India, 2 for East Africa, 3 for the southern whale fishery. The subscribers present authorized them to raise another million for the outfits.

In November 1781 Bolts fitted out a ship, the *Cobenzel*, for the north-west coast of America, for the trade in otter furs with China— a new trade just discovered by Captain Cook. The ship was to round Cape Horn, take in furs at Nootka, sell in China, and return by the Cape—the first Austrian circumnavigation.

He engaged four English officers, bred under Cook, and five naturalists; bought a Bermudian sloop as a tender, and got recommendations from the Emperor to various Princes, at whose ports the ship would touch. The intrigues of his fellow Directors at Vienna and Trieste wrecked his scheme and caused enormous loss.

By April 1782 the Antwerp Directors had six million florins and six ships at work under Austrian colours, but their factory at Delagoa was destroyed by the Portuguese, who claimed sovereignty and commercial monopoly of the east coast of Africa.

In 1784 five of the Company's vessels arrived from China at Ostend, since 1781 a free port, with $3\frac{1}{2}$ million pounds of tea. But in the same year they lost the *Imperial Eagle*, a ship built for them at Trieste at a cost of 300,000 florins, which was arrested, with her cargo, in Cadiz harbour by their creditors—a loss of 290,000 florins. A panic of the shareholders followed, and their shares fell 38 per cent. below par.

At the close of 1784 the Company became bankrupt at Antwerp for 10 million florins.

The failure of this Company, who seem to have met with scarcely any foreign opposition,[1] except from the feeble East India Govern-

---

[1] In July 1784, however, we find the Bombay Government refusing the request of the Commander of the Imperial ship *L'Autrichien* for permission to land her cargo at Bombay. But when he repeated his request, laying stress on the assistance he had tendered and given to British ships and officials, the Council, with one dissentient, withdrew their previous refusal and allowed the stores to be landed.

ment of Portugal, may be chiefly ascribed to the jealousy and mis-understanding between Bolts and his colleagues at Antwerp.   He seems also to have had too much of the dashing spirit of a projector ; and they, though the principals in point of capital, appear to have been entirely destitute of the particular kind of knowledge requisite for conducting a trade with India.

CHAPTER VII

CONTEMPORARY WRITERS ON MR BOLTS

IN the year 1782 the various calumnies which were being industriously circulated in the English press against the reputation of Warren Hastings by secret agents of his malignant and unscrupulous enemy Francis were presented to the public in a single work entitled "Travels in Europe, Asia, etc.," by W. M. The writer was a worthless adventurer, named William MacIntosh, the half-caste son of a Scotsman and a French bride, whose knavery was relentlessly exposed in a tract written by Captain Joseph Price in the same year and reprinted in 1783. MacIntosh's work, a clever "olla podrida" of all the recent writers on Indian topics, is in the form of a series of letters, one of which he had the impudence to address to Lord North, an audacious stroke which indicates pretty clearly the hand of Junius in the venture. Letter No. 37, dated Calcutta the 28th October 1779, after seriously proposing "a partition of the sovereignty of Hindustan between Great Britain and the Emperor," proceeds to show how such a policy should be carried out with reference to the various Powers of India, European and native, and makes the following observations on the case of Mr Bolts :

"The injustice done to Mr William Bolts, in refusing to his British creditors, after he was declared a bankrupt in England, the benefit and indulgence of the Company's constitution, that they might recover to their own uses the debts owing to him by natives, under pretence that the trade whereby the debts were contracted was contrary to the Company's bye-laws,[1] will vindicate on his part the indulgence of a disposition naturally vindictive, while he wreaks his vengeance at the only period and in the only place where his knowledge and genius were able to gain credit and confidence. Driven to the last extremity of distress, he was supported by British subjects in London: patronised by them, he offered his services to the Court of Lisbon, but they were not accepted.   Disappointed in his views in Portugal, he accidentally procured a commission from the Court of Vienna, to form commercial establishments in Asia. A speculative, inventive, and persevering genius like Mr Bolts might have succeeded in the character of coadjutor to M. St Lubin in his negotiations for France with the Marrattas and Hyder Ally, and have formed a coalition between the German Emperor and the King of France dangerous in the highest degree to the British interest in Hindostan.[2]   But, as a speculative merchant, he must have sunk under accumulated losses and charges, and could never have returned to Leghorn, Triest, or Vienna, had not some of the principal members of the Company's own Government in Bombay and Madras furnished him with the means of sending proofs of his abilities, and of the performance of his promises, in three large ships, completely laden, under Imperial colours into the Mediterranean.   With this countenance and assistance he has erected about six flag staffs, on which Imperial colours are occasionally displayed, on the coasts of Malabar and Coromandel: the Car-Niccobars claimed by Denmark, and Rio de la Goa on the south-east coast of Africa.   The assistance afforded to Mr Bolts by the Company's servants, and creditable houses in trade under the Company's protection, was a violation of positive orders from the Court of Directors, which were published in the several presidencies.   A conduct so injurious and even so insolent calls aloud for censure. To deprive the delinquents of their offices would be the most mild and at the same time the most effectual method of defeating the success of Mr Bolts's schemes and operations in Hindostan hereafter; and at the same time, of rendering persons in the service, or under the protection of the East India Company, more tender of breaking through their orders and sacrificing their political rights in future."

---

[1] " There was a palpable impropriety in a high and respectable corporation's descending to show personal resentment against an alien, who had been forced to dismiss himself from their service and had been disgracefully removed from their settlements for notorious offences."

[2] There can be no doubt that the view here expressed is sound.   In letter 59, however, with ridiculous inconsistency, the writer pooh-poohs the intrigues of St Lubin, and declares the notion that he negotiated a treaty with the Mahrattas to be a mere chimera !

In a despatch of the 29th of August 1781 the Directors report the seizure of the ship *Great Duke of Tuscany*, under Tuscan colours, an English vessel bought by Mr Bolts since the commencement of the war with France, with a valuable cargo from the coast of Coromandel. She was seized at the Cape by two French frigates, and condemned by them, the Dutch Governor not choosing to interfere. The Governor-General and his Council are directed to make a strict and particular enquiry

"whether any and who of our servants or persons under our protection were concerned in the above ship bought by Mr Bolts, or had any interest therein which occasioned her condemnation, as also to make the most minute enquiry who of our servants or persons under our protection had any concerns or transactions in the promotion of any trade carried on by foreigners or in furnishing them by any means with ships or vessels for the purpose of carrying on such trade or otherwise."

In his tract entitled "Some observations . . . on . . . Travels in Europe, etc.," Captain Price has some remarks on the literary work of Colonel Dow and Count Bolts, and commenting on the vindictiveness attributed to the latter by MacIntosh, observes :

"I would likewise have had him more tender of the Chevalier St Lubin's character, as well as that of Mr Bolts ; neither of them, as I ever heard, having stabbed in the dark, or by the means of initials, men's characters who had cloathed, fed, and cherished them. Can Mr Macintosh say so much ? Mr Francis and General Smith might do well to ask him that question."

On a later page of the tract he ridicules MacIntosh's extraordinary assertion that Haidar Ali had been a frequent visitor to his ship while he was lying off Mangalore, and continues :

"Mangalore . . . is a sea-port town on the coast of Malabar . . . not the capital of Hyder Ally's dominions. . . . As to his putting the French in possession of it, or even permitting them to hoist a flag, as the Portuguese, Danes, Dutch, and even Count Bolts has been permitted to do, it is no such thing."

From these two references, apparently made in good faith and not ironically, to the position of Mr Bolts, it appears that he had at this time assumed the title of a Count of the Holy Roman Empire. Whether the Emperor Joseph had really conferred such a title on him there seems to be no evidence in the English records to show : if so, the fact was unknown to the writer of the brief sketch of his life contained in the "Biographie Universelle," published in 1812, which, with slight modifications, has been utilised in several other dictionaries of biography. On the other hand, it is prima facie improbable that Mr Bolts would have risked the Imperial favour by assuming a rank to which he was not entitled ; and he was too well known a personage to assume it without attracting immediate attention.

In an anonymous pamphlet of 1783, "The Saddle put on the Right Horse, or an enquiry into the Reason why certain persons have been denominated Nabobs," the author gives an imaginary conversation between himself and a Bengali gentleman, in which the latter says :

"As for Mr Bolts, he was what we call a thorough bred merchant, whose predominant passion was the love of gain ; to that principle he sacrificed everything. You must have heard that he has written to his Banyan, and other country merchants here, that his affairs are turned out so bad, that he has been obliged to become bankrupt—and so pay all his debts at once. This news makes his friends ——— and ——— look white ; for he owes to them and their dependents three hundred and forty thousand rupees on bond. But I do not like to talk of him. You know how infamous we think the character of a man, who acted so base a part as he did."

Author. "You are right, Sir ; but even he, contemptible as he is, has met with patrons in England, where we English gentlemen of Asia seem to have been proscribed in the lump." When Dow's third volume was in the press, the writer says, "an idea had been taken up by the Minister of the day to claim the territory held by the East India Company in behalf of the Crown. . . . To this end, and to prejudice the nation against the Company, Bolts was encouraged in his infamous publications. Dow was flattered, and induced to permit some plans, schemes, and general reflections, to be bound up in his third volume." I suspect that Philip Francis was behind both Dow and Bolts. Burke alludes to both writers in his "Observations on a late state of the Nation": "Dow's insinuations of secret murders, and Bolts's unjust statements of the inadequateness of the Mayor's Court to an equal distribution of justice to the English inhabitants of Calcutta in Bengal."

CHAPTER VIII

LAST YEARS

LITTLE information can be gleaned from the records of the subsequent history of Mr Bolts. When the Empress Maria Theresa died in 1780, her son and successor, the Emperor Joseph II., continued at first to favour him, but eventually revoked the commission as Lieut.-Colonel which Mr Bolts had held for several years. Mr Bolts appears to have divided his time between Europe and the East until the collapse of the Imperial Company towards the end of the year 1784. In a general letter from Bengal of 5th April 1783, after a reference to the Directors' orders of 14th January 1780, the Council remarks:

"After being forbid any intercourse with Mr Bolts, and having issued the prohibition of trade with him generally to all Dependants of this Government, it was not in our power to admit of any goods imported in his name being passed through the Custom House."

In paragraph 27 of the same letter we read:

"Mr Bolts. Letter of representation was presented from him; but we did not think ourselves at liberty to receive it."

This question of the detention of some timber belonging to Mr Bolts seems to have dragged on for many years:

"At a meeting of the Directors held on the 8th of October, 1800 a letter dated the 7th October was read, in which he requested to be paid the sum of £2569/12/6 the value of a lot of redwood, his property, which was sold by mistake at the Custom-house at Calcutta, and the amount paid in to the Company's treasury there."

The letter was referred to the Committee of Correspondence. On the 26th of November 1800, on a report from the Committee of Correspondence being read, it was resolved

"That Mr William Bolts be allowed the sum of £256–19–6, being the prime cost of redwood, his property, which was sold by mistake at the Custom-House at Calcutta . . . on his giving a discharge in full of all demands upon the Company, and that a warrant be made out for the same accordingly."

The fact that Mr Bolts's letter of the 7th October was received next day shows that he was then in London.

From 1784—except for the above extracts—Mr Bolts s name disappears from the Council Minutes. All that seems to be known of him after this date is that he was in France in 1808, probably engaged in fresh intrigues against the East India Company,[1] and that he died that year in a hospital at Paris, "in great poverty," says Van der Aa.

[1] "Twice possessed of great wealth, he tried his fortune again by creating an establishment near Paris. The war with England again destroyed his hopes" (MacIntosh, "Vindiciæ Gallicæ").

APPENDIX

PETITION TO THE GRAND JURY

THE following is the text of Mr Bolts's Petition to the Grand Jury:

"To the Jurors of our Sovereign Lord the King for the Town and Districts of Calcutta now assembled. The Information and Petition of William Bolts, Inhabitant and Householder of the said Town of Calcutta.

Humbly sheweth

That your Petitioner is a freeman and Loyal Subject of Great Britain who in the year 1759 entered into the service of the Honourable the United Company of merchants of England trading to the East Indies under covenants for five years, and by virtue of the authority aforesaid came out to Bengal where he faithfully served the said Company for a much longer term than he engaged for; That having resigned the said Honourable Company's service he has since continued to reside in Calcutta as a merchant, in which profession he has always had very weighty and considerable mercantile concerns which he has ever transacted as he humbly hopes with honor to himself, with peace and satisfaction respecting the community without infringement of the Laws of his Country and without having ever acted contrary to the interests of the East India Company; That your Petitioner has frequently since his resignation of the service had the honor of serving upon the Grand Jury and of acting as one of His Majesty's Judges in the Honourable the Mayor's Court of this town to which he was legally appointed by the President and Council, and in which station he has still the honor to continue; That your Petitioner has recently received very positive evidence and information which he will support by his own corporal oath and the oaths of good and lawful witnesses that on or about the 4th day of May inst. within the Districts of this Town of Calcutta aforesaid one Richard Smith[1]

---

[1] Colonel Richard Smith had taken a prominent part in urging the Council to proceed to extremities with Mr Bolts, both in his letter of the

at present residing within the jurisdiction aforesaid, Colonel and Commander-in-Chief of the Troops in the service of the aforesaid East India Company, with other persons at present to your Petitioner unknown did then and there associate and hold an illegal conspiracy against the person of your said Petitioner; That the said Conspirators then and there against the peace of our Lord the King his Crown and Dignity, against the form of the statutes, and in open defiance of the Charter granted the East India Company, but particularly in contempt of the Great Charter the great foundation of the Liberties of our Constitution called the Magna Charta, whereby it is particularly stipulated that no freeman shall be imprisoned or disseized of his freehold, did maliciously combine by force to seize and imprison the body of your Petitioner and to put him on board some ship and send him beyond seas, which Resolution the said Conspirators have agreed to and resolved among themselves in writing to adhere to and carry into execution, That your Petitioner is therefore in fear of his Life, or in case he should escape with Life upon the execution of such an execrable plan that he and his family are in danger of being ruined with many other British subjects who have entrusted their Property in your Petitioner's hands, which together with his own will amount to upwards of one hundred and ten thousand pounds sterling and which is what your Petitioner has actually under his management in different parts of India as his Books will evince.

That your Petitioner is informed that the principal Conspirator Richard Smith aforesaid proposes to quit Calcutta, and as the present sessions is actually sitting and does not admit of time for application to a Justice of Peace which in the present case this Petitioner is informed is unnecessary, your Petitioner therefore has been advised to prefer his Information to the unbiassed judgment of the Jurors now solemnly assembled.

Wherefore he the said humble Petitioner solemnly conjures and calls upon you the said Jurors by the sacred oaths which you have just taken and by all the sacred ties of Divine and your Country's Laws to take him and his family under your Protection and to pursue such methods in his behalf as may secure his Person and Property from said inhuman and illegal acts intended to be perpetrated against him by the said Conspirator Richard Smith and his accessaries, that he and every one of them may be this sessions jointly and separately bound over to the Peace and upon conviction be obliged to give Special Bail for their future good behaviour with good securities for the before said sum of one hundred and ten thousand pounds sterling and other damages which may accrue to

---

11th of December 1767 (see page 58) and in a subsequent Minute of the 4th of May 1768.

your Petitioner should the said Richard Smith illegally make use of the Military force under his command to carry into execution the atrocious Resolves of himself and accessaries.

And your Petitioner as in duty bound shall ever pray

WILLIAM BOLTS.

CALCUTTA TOWN HALL
27 *May* 1768."

INDEX

plain